HEROES
Among Us

HEROES
Among Us

Ordinary People,

Extraordinary Choices

JOHN QUIÑONES
with Stephen P. Williams

HARPER

An Imprint of HarperCollins*Publishers*
www.harpercollins.com

HarperCollins books may be purchased for educational, business, or sales promotional use. For information, please write: Special Markets Department, HarperCollins Publishers, 10 East 53rd Street, New York, NY 10022.

FIRST EDITION

Designed by Jaime Putorti

Library of Congress Cataloging-in-Publication Data is available upon request.

ISBN: 978-0-06-173360-4

08 09 10 11 12 DIX/RRD 10 9 8 7 6 5 4 3 2 1

For my children, Nicco, Andrea, and Julian,
whose love, joy, and compassion never cease to amaze me.

—JQ

In spite of everything, I still believe that
people are really good at heart.

—Anne Frank

The smallest good deed is better than
the grandest good intention.

—Duguet

Contents

HEROES
Among Us

CHAPTER ONE

Heroes Everywhere

On a Saturday morning, at a bakery near Waco, Texas, I found a display of bigotry as fresh as the coffee and pastries people stopped in to buy.

A young Muslim woman dressed in a traditional headscarf ordered a pastry from the man behind the counter.

"You'll have to leave," he told her.

"What do you mean?" the woman asked politely.

"We don't serve camel jockeys in here," he said.

Several customers milled about the store, looking uncomfortable, trying not to pay attention. I was watching all this on TV monitors in a room in the back of the bakery. Both the Muslim woman and the man behind the counter were actors and hidden cameras were rolling. It was all part of the TV show I host for ABC News called *What Would You Do?*

"You won't serve me?" asked the woman, seemingly dumbfounded.

"How do I know you don't have a bomb in that bag?" the man behind the counter retorted.

"This is outrageous," said the woman playing the part of a Muslim.

I watched in astonishment what happened next. An older man approached and gave our man behind the counter an emphatic thumbs-up. "Good job," he said. "I like the way you dealt with her." Then he took his bag of donuts and left.

It was a scene I was ashamed to have witnessed.

Moments later, in the parking lot with a camera crew in tow, I caught up with this man as he climbed into his pickup truck.

"Excuse me, sir," I said. "My name is John Quiñones."

But before I could ask him a single question, he jumped out of his truck, jabbed his finger in my face and snapped: "You're not an American."

That hit me hard.

I'm a native, sixth-generation American. But it's true I grew up in segregation, in the barrio. I'd known where "my place" was, and that was on the west side of San Antonio. The north side of the city, which was mostly white, was pretty much forbidden to someone who looked like me. These were the unspoken rules of my childhood, and now I was hearing them loud and clear.

After a short break, we reset the scene.

On cue, our Muslim actress approached the counter and asked to buy a sweet roll. Again, the actor playing the bigoted man behind the counter refused to serve her.

"How do I know you're not a terrorist?" he taunted her. "You're dressed like one."

"Excuse me?" said the actress playing our Muslim.

"Look, take your jihad back out to the parking lot. I've got to protect my customers," the clerk said.

This time we noticed two young women customers—one of whom later turned out to be Muslim, although her typical Texas clothing gave no indication of this—who stopped in their tracks. They were staring, their mouths wide open, incredulous. Finally, one of them mustered the courage to speak up.

"You're really offensive," she practically shouted at the clerk.

Her friend joined in: "You're disgusting."

They stood their ground and demanded to speak to the clerk's manager. Even though they'd never met the woman who was being abused, her cause was theirs.

Watching these women stand up for what they believed in made me proud to live in a country where people are willing to risk getting into a fight, or worse, to defend a stranger being bullied. The millions of viewers who tune in to watch *What Would You Do?* each week get a thrill from seeing everyday heroes like these women in action. And, as the anchor of the show, I get the same thrill.

The confrontation in Waco wouldn't be my last encounter with intolerance and bigotry. A year later, at a delicatessen in New Jersey, I myself jumped into the fray. As customers looked on I pretended to be a Mexican day laborer and, speaking in broken English, tried to order a sandwich. Again, the man behind the counter was an actor. "Speak English or take your pesos down the road," he snapped.

"Por favor," I pleaded. "Café con un sandwich."

"We're building a wall to keep you people out," he shouted. "We don't serve illegals here."

Even though I knew it was all an act, the words cut through me like a knife.

I asked the other customers for help. But each one turned away, giving me the cold shoulder.

"I don't speak Mexican," they said time and again.

One customer not only agreed with our racist man behind the counter, but also told me if I didn't leave, he would throw me out of the deli himself or call the cops.

But then, just when I thought no one would step up against racism, the tide turned. All it took were the words of one compassionate customer

"He's a human being just like you and me," she said.

Immediately, the crowd joined in, angrily berating the racist proprietor. "This is America! We're a melting pot. Maybe you're the one who should leave!"

Finally, people with the courage to face down bigotry. It was as though someone had pulled the knife out.

If you ask me, that's what heroism is all about. Most people think it involves dramatic events and near superhuman feats of courage. I have found that this is not the case at all.

There are so many problems and challenges in the world

today and, as a TV journalist, I see more than my share. But lately, I find myself seeking out everyday heroes, people looking to make the world a better place. I think we're all searching for them, in some way or another. And I find them wherever I go.

True heroism is remarkably sober, very undramatic. It is not the urge to surpass all others at whatever cost, but the urge to serve others at whatever cost.

—Arthur Ashe

My family has been in the United States almost two hundred years. But in many ways, the first five generations of the Quiñones family never left Mexico behind, even as they embraced the Stars and Stripes, served in the military, and paid their taxes. If you'd ever run into my mother, Maria, down in San Antonio, you might have thought she was visiting from the old country. Given her limited English and Indian features, if she were alive today many people would probably try to have her deported.

Thanks to her, I've traveled light-years from my childhood. And thanks to her that childhood remains rooted within me, giving me strength, direction, and faith. My mom was definitely my first hero. She taught me to be open enough to believe in the world's goodness, to believe in people. She taught me how to observe and learn and, in this way, I've taught myself, and now others, that there are heroes among us.

※

I was born in 1952, on the west side of San Antonio. When my parents brought me home from the hospital, the first thing my mother did was say a prayer at her shrine of the Virgin of Guadalupe, the patron saint of Mexico. She'd lovingly assembled this intricate monument in the foyer of our tiny bungalow. It was a beautiful thing, maybe five feet tall, with a couple of crucifixes, enough candles to light a house, and a ceramic Virgin with her hands clasped in prayer. It wouldn't have looked out of place in the niche of some grand cathedral. At the time, I believed it was the kind of thing everybody had in their homes. Obviously, I had much to learn.

The Virgin was my mother's hero and a source of her guiding light. To her, the Virgin represented strength and hope. And this light, the one my mother taught me to look for in people, is the one that continues to guide me. I see this light all the time. It's not the stereotype one sees in movies when a person is called by the divine to rise up to heaven, nor the golden glow that surrounds an angel in a Renaissance painting. This light is nothing like that. It's this light that I see when someone picks up a ten-dollar bill for a person who hadn't realized they had dropped it. It is present when someone says, "excuse me" on the subway, or "thank you" to the barista at a busy Starbucks. I feel this light when a total stranger offers me a genuine smile for no reason at all.

I suppose I grew up poor. And surely, by today's standards, where everyone wants to be a star and drive a Beamer, we were far from rich. But I never felt deprived. My father, Bruno, a mostly silent man, dropped out of school after completing the third grade. He worked a variety of jobs for the rest of his life. He picked cotton at one point. He lost his finger in a wood chipper at another. He dug ditches. But, mainly, he was a janitor. And, on weekends, I would help him manicure the lawns of rich folks on the north side of town. We were paid twenty-five dollars per lawn and a little extra for trimming the trees. My father always put in those extra days to help the family. And he took great pride in his work.

My mother only made it through the eighth grade. She cleaned houses—also on the north side of town—when she wasn't making sure our own home was spotless. I never heard my parents complain or whine about their jobs. I never heard them wish they had been born in different circumstances. My dad's sole purpose in life was to provide for us. And my mom's was to care for us. That was what success meant to them.

Now, there are days I can get caught up in the daily grind (we all do), so caught up that I'll get upset about something small, such as not getting a clear signal on my cell phone at the airport, or someone cutting ahead of me in line. None of which ultimately matters. It sometimes seems that we've made our lives so complicated in our search for pleasure and ease that we forget what's truly important. At these moments, when I think I'm just going to lose it, I remember my parents' daily grind, their lives. How their days were so different from my own. They never had a BlackBerry break down on them nor had their flight to Aruba delayed due to bad weather. They rarely ventured outside the world of their parents. And yet, although their lives seemed simple, I envy how connected they were to their honor, their dignity, their family, without these distractions. Their centered lives make sense to me now in ways I couldn't have comprehended when I was a kid, or perhaps even five years ago. Their example is the driving force that empowers me, and it is reflected in the heroes I meet today. I see now that my parents are heroes because they put others—my sisters, me, the neighbor kids, and stray animals, anyone who needed help—before themselves.

Mom made our rickety bungalow on Arizona Street seem like the center of the universe. She treated the place as if it were our palace. Like many older Texas homes, ours was a wood-frame house built on rock pilings that created a small space where, as a child, I would play games and hide. In the winter, when the cold air blew up from the floorboards, mom would fire up the gas-powered space heaters. If she was feeling flush, she'd send me down to the corner store for some Mexican chocolate, which she'd whip into hot milk to make cocoa.

My sisters, Irma and Rosemary, shared one of only two bedrooms in the bungalow. My parents had the other. During the first ten years of my life, I slept on a cot in my parents' room. When I got older, I slept on the living room couch. In those first years, we didn't have a shower or a bathtub. To bathe, we'd heat up some water, pour it into a large basin, and scrub ourselves down. Then we'd dump the dirty water in the backyard and refill it for the next person. Mornings were a long, drawn-out affair in my childhood home.

Remembering this from the vantage point of my apartment, which overlooks the glittering lights of Manhattan, I find this memory incredible. But back then, it was just life. The whole neighborhood contained small wooden bungalows with basins for bathtubs, filled with Mexican-American families like mine that minded their business and kept their heads down. Until duty called. And, as I'm learning, at some point in everyone's life, duty always calls.

My mom was certain I'd do big things. I guess all mothers think this of their children. But mine was absolutely convinced. I don't know why she felt so strongly. I wasn't an exceptional child. Even though I was born in the U.S., we only spoke Spanish at home. I didn't speak English until I started public school. This limited me to the life I saw my father living—doing jobs that only represented putting food on your family's table, with no thought of a career. Frankly, given how many fathers don't even do that, my father seems quite the hero in comparison. He'd never have seen it that way—he was only doing what he was supposed to do. But isn't this absence of drama, after all, part of what makes a hero?

On the first day I walked into class at Carvajal Elementary School, I didn't understand a word the teacher was saying. Bilingual education wasn't even a dream back then. It was sink or swim. Most of us eventually sank. I remember the class got up and filed out the door after a couple of hours. Not knowing what was going on, I followed them out. I made my way back home, relieved that it was all over so quickly. School isn't so bad, I thought.

"What are you doing back home so soon?" my mother asked, her face filled with concern.

"School's over," I said. "She let us all go."

"What? It's just recess. A break. Get back there now!"

So I went back. And tried to learn a few words. At lunch, as the other kids were pulling out their Wonder Bread sandwiches, I dug into the flour tortilla and bean tacos my mother had packed, all the while marveling at the exotic lunches around me.

When I got home, my mom was impressed with my one new word in English: *baloney*.

"It's a start," she said, shrugging her shoulders.

And she was right.

Our simple life felt good. It felt right. I learned that if you watch your step, and eventually take a leap toward something, anything is possible. And my mother made sure I took that leap.

A mother is not a person to lean on but a person
to make leaning unnecessary.

—Dorothy Canfield Fisher

After elementary school, I moved on to Rhodes Middle School because we thought we had no other option. We couldn't afford a parochial school and I doubt any of the fancy private schools in San Antonio would have accepted a Mexican boy like me, let alone offered me the scholarship I would need to attend. The middle school was just a hundred yards down the street from the elementary school I had gone to, and through sheer convenience, it was my next educational step.

Across the street from the school was a housing project, a grim collection of brick buildings we called The Courts. Many mornings I'd walk to school and come across a discarded brown paper lunch bag. It wasn't litter. It was paraphernalia. If you peered inside one, you'd find crystallized goo on the bottom. "Glue heads" sniffed this model airplane cement on their way to school in the morning. These kids would get totally messed up on the stuff before class. The beginning of shenanigans they'd pull throughout the day. There were drive-by shootings, stabbings, and fistfights.

But still, it was school. I wasn't a glue head and I had a family that loved me. So I was able to learn. School was where I first realized I could write to express myself. And think.

Frustrated at the dismal future ahead of them, many kids my age found refuge in gangs, crime, and violence. In an irony I could never shake, my neighborhood was ruled by a gang called Ghost Town. I guess their way of life made them see their surroundings (and people like me) as dead and empty, much like the ominous name they fought so ruthlessly to defend.

Still, they couldn't stop me from setting my sights high even when it looked like I would never get out of the barrio. The worst of times for the Quiñoneses came in 1966 when my father was laid off from work. As the weeks went by with zero income, my father and mother made the tough decision to do what many other Mexican families did: we would become migrant farm workers. We had no choice. We joined a caravan of migrants and journeyed from San Antonio to Northport, Michigan, to pick cherries. After a couple of months of teetering on ladders for seventy-five cents for every bucket of cherries, we then followed the harvest to Swanson, Ohio. There, we hit the tomato orchards where I became a champion picker, filling a hundred bushels a day. At thirty-five cents per basket, that was thirty-five dollars. Not a bad contribution to the family fund.

It was the longest summer of my life. But I learned a valuable lesson: I didn't want to do that forever. I was more determined to stay in school and try to go to college. Not that anyone else thought I could.

When I finally returned to my middle school in San Antonio, the general attitude was, "Okay, these kids are Mexican, let's send them to wood or metal shop, or have them study auto mechanics." The principal, Mr. Runnels, was Anglo—which is what we called anyone who spoke grammatically correct English—and so were the teachers. None of them spoke Spanish. Most of the local families simply went along with the idea that their kids were destined to be grease monkeys, or laborers. And it's not surprising that most of us followed along. We rarely saw any successful people of color on TV. And in my world, all we had was the Frito Bandito and Speedy Gonzales. With such low expectations, we kids from the barrio tended to fulfill the stereotypes. No ambition. No smarts. No good. To be expected.

My mother never saw it this way. In my seventh grade shop class, I made her a coffee table with a tile-inlay portrait of the Virgin of Guadalupe. Mom made the sign of the cross whenever she passed it. And heaven forbid you set a cup of coffee on it. Although she loved that table, and it went perfectly with the inspirational motif of her prayer altar, my mother wasn't going to let me go the vocational route. She had *sueños grandes*— big dreams—for me.

Fortunately, while I had inherited my mother's Indian features—thus my nickname Chino, because my Indian face looked Asian when I squinted—I'd also been blessed with the big and tall conquistador blood that so many northern Mexicans share. People thought twice before picking a fight with me. Obviously, they didn't know what a gentle giant I was. At the end of the day, I was more scared of my mother than I was of any gang.

But once I was in class, I could forget about much of what happened on the streets. I actually liked school. And I grew to love theater. I even played Romeo in Shakespeare's *Romeo and Juliet*. My best buddy, Don Cortez, who still lives in the old barrio and is still my good friend, played my sidekick, Mercutio. We performed for the entire school district at the downtown Municipal Auditorium. Pretty fancy for a couple of kids who would get run out of the white neighborhoods if we tried to walk through them without a lawnmower and some hedge clippers in tow.

"FORMER MIGRANT WORKER GETS TO PLAY ROMEO AND LATER BECOMES NETWORK TV ANCHORMAN." It sounds like a headline from a rags-to-riches story. Only in America. But then again, mine is truly the all-American story. How did it happen? A lot of hard work, a family that never gave up on me, and maybe a little luck along the way. But, in the end, I'm where I am today because of all the opportunities available in this country, and because I've taken to heart just what it means to be an American.

Within this book, you will find stories that will impress, awe, and inspire you. I know I felt that way when I wrote it. Telling these stories just made me admire the heroes I've met over the years even more. Sprinkled throughout these pages, you'll find some quotes I've jotted down in my notebooks over the years to remember the thoughts of people I've admired. I turn to their words often to show me the way. I hope you find them as helpful to you as they have been to me.

I've included some quizzes based on real-life scenarios of ethically challenging situations. Try these multiple-choice questions and see how you rate as a hero; the answers may surprise you.

There's also a chapter titled "Our Hall of Heroes," which

I'm particularly proud of. This chapter includes short biographies of individuals who really touched me through their lives and deeds. Read about them and ponder how truly powerful a dedicated and courageous person can be in this world.

I feel privileged to have had the opportunity to meet so many amazing people, and to share their stories with the millions of viewers of *What Would You Do?* In this book, I will share some of the best stories from the show, and from my life as a journalist and an American. All the people in this book are ordinary folks who've done extraordinary things when confronted with life's unpredictable, challenging situations.

I've found that even in the midst of hardship, wars, economic stresses, natural disasters, and other tough circumstances, American heroes shine through. They're Christian, Muslim, Mexican, African American, European, and more. They're black, white, brown, and every shade in between. They're women and men, grown-ups, and kids. They're the type of people who will jump out of their car and run into flames, without even thinking, to save your life in a freeway accident. They're the retired women who step boldly into the fray when they see teenagers harassing a homeless man. Their ethical courage transcends their fear. They're everywhere in America.

And thank goodness for that.

CHAPTER TWO

Those Who Take Action

I recall the construction of that tower as though it were yesterday.

Walking to school each day I would gaze up into the distance, amazed at the progress the workers made. In the barrio where I lived, nothing went higher than thirty feet, yet here were some men raising something that seemed as though it could literally touch the sky.

The city of San Antonio had begun building the 750-foot Tower of the Americas, which was to make its debut at the 1968 World's Fair. The loud booms from the jackhammers and cranes could be heard for miles. I was only twelve years old.

I remember daydreaming about living at the top of that tower one day. It seemed unattainable, beyond reach. And yet it was inspirational to me. For a kid who had never ventured outside San Antonio, that tower, reaching more than seventy stories into the sky, meant anything was possible. Even now, forty years later, I realize that in my young imagination it stood for something: a bigger world out there waiting to be conquered.

I remember charting the progress of that tower from the ball fields outside my old junior high. As it rose, so did my hopes of one day leaving Texas. Not because I hated Texas or had a terrible childhood, but because, as that tower rose, I became convinced of what my mother always told me: I was capable of anything. I mattered. We all mattered.

The city architects had designed and manufactured a massive disc-shaped restaurant and observation deck to sit at the top of the tower. It seemed miraculous when, one day in October 1967, they set about hoisting this huge structure to the top. Just as it looked like everything was set, some cables snapped, partially loosening its massive top-house. For a time it hung precariously, a looming failure.

That spoke to me. I, too, was at a precarious point in my life. Growing up in a rough section of San Antonio, I could easily forget that I could get ahead in the world. Most of us west-side kids were told quite the opposite. And if we didn't hear such pessimism at first, many people certainly made sure that negative message reached us, again and again.

Eventually, they got the observation deck in place. And I moved on. It's odd that now, many years later, I live on the twenty-eighth floor of a Manhattan high-rise. It may not be the 1968 Tower of the Americas as envisioned by the city of San Antonio, but it is the tower that I always envisioned myself living in one day; I finally got to the top. And the fact that it's so far from the one that I first dreamed of doesn't really matter at all.

When I think about what got me here, I remember my parents, my teachers, the various people in my life who went out of their way to give me a boost. I accepted their help with humility. And when I got the chance to work, I worked as hard and as well as I could, whether it was picking cherries in a migrant labor camp when I was a boy or standing before the network cameras on live TV. My story, at its heart, is not so very different from the stories of the people I've covered throughout my career.

In my decades as a journalist, I've traveled to every state and dozens of countries, meeting people and learning about cultures I would never have dreamed I'd ever come to know. In the process, I have encountered many unlikely heroes. I've often wondered what it takes for someone to cross the chasm and become one.

I do realize that many people can't always react as heroes. That's not something one should judge harshly. It's just a fact. These days, everyone is looking to Hollywood celebrities, politicians, and other supposed leading lights for guidance and a plan (preferably an easy one) to get what they want. Sure, some of these people are wise. But the truth is the greatest inspiration is often right in front of us. We just have to pay attention. We must train ourselves to see. And then to act.

Occasionally you come across someone who steps up and becomes a hero. I'm lucky in my work. I get to see people doing the right thing all the time. My childhood was shaped by a handful of wonderful, compassionate teachers.

Teresa Gutierrez, my English teacher, came into my life in the tenth grade at Brackenridge High School. I remember that my school counselors, at the time, kept telling me I wasn't college material. It was the same "guidance" they gave to most of my fellow Latino students. But Ms. Gutierrez was different. She had noticed I was a good writer and insisted that I join the staff as a reporter for the school newspaper, the *Brackenridge Times*. My career as a journalist was born. Ms. Gutierrez taught me to pursue my dreams, however lofty.

Sharon Christa Corrigan McAuliffe was the same kind of teacher. And I'll never forget covering her valor firsthand.

Born in 1948, Christa, as she was called, became a high school social studies teacher in Concord, New Hampshire, in 1982. As a kid, she was inspired by the space race and the quest to send an American to the moon. So when NASA invited teachers to apply for a slot on the space shuttle, she submitted an application. Amazingly, she was selected out of eleven thousand other applicants to fly on the space shuttle *Challenger*. NASA had been looking for a teacher who could connect and communicate with kids around the world. They'd certainly found the right person in Christa. She had devoted her life to teaching, and now she was making the trip to space in an effort to take her work that giant step further.

In 1985 she took a year's leave of absence to train for the

'86 liftoff. Her smiling face and obvious courage appealed to everyone, and soon she was on the airwaves, being interviewed by everyone from Larry King to David Letterman. The media loved her. And the whole world, including many, many school-children, tuned in to watch the shuttle's takeoff on January 28, 1986.

"What are we doing here? We're reaching for the stars," she said, when asked why she was going into space.

I was at the Kennedy Space Center with her parents on that sunny day in January 1986. I remember how excited they were as the engines of the shuttle's booster rockets fired up, the orange blasts preparing to lift their daughter into the blue Florida sky and beyond.

"Stay on their faces," I told the cameraman as liftoff commenced. Her parents looked so proud, and I wanted America to see that.

Seventy-three seconds later, the shuttle exploded into a cloud of debris. Christa's parent's faces went from joy to pride to confusion to shock to devastation. They were quickly whisked away. I was so upset I began shaking as I reported live on the tragedy. And my anchorman at the time, Peter Jennings, even had to tell me during a break that I was too emotional and needed to calm down. He was right. But I could barely contain myself. Christa represented hope to many of us. She reminded us of all the teachers that we had, the kind that asked us to dream by challenging ourselves. To me, Christa was a true hero. She got into the space program at the last minute, against all odds. Schoolchildren across the country had tuned in just to watch her lift off. Many hearts were broken that day.

In retrospect, I can see that even though her death was a tragedy of unimaginable proportions, her example remains an inspiration to millions of people around the world. She certainly is one of mine. I'll never forget one thing she said: "Reach for it. Push yourself as far as you can. And never give up. Never."

She'd climbed to the ultimate heights and I understood what she was saying. I'd climbed, too, in my own way.

Her legacy perseveres. Dozens of schools have been named after Christa. Roads and highways bear her name. Movies and documentaries have been made about her life. And there's even a Christa McAuliffe Technology Conference each year in Nashua, New Hampshire, which focuses on technological developments for education. "I touch the future. I teach," Christa said.

Her words still resonate with me. So often teachers go way beyond their job description without adequate pay and often without accolades from parents or the community. I'm sure you'll be hard-pressed to find any educator motivated by money and praise.

"To the world you may be one person, but to one person you may be the world."

—Anonymous

Take the case of Heather Collins, a special-education high school teacher near the Arizona-Nevada border. Her classes usually include about twenty kids, some of whom are physically disabled and coping with learning disorders and other mental disabilities. While Heather is mandated to teach them their ABCs, and get them through the school's curriculum, she takes their education quite a few steps further.

Heather teaches her students the life skills they need to survive as adults. She teaches them to think and act practically. She wants her kids to be self-sufficient, to be able to make their way in the world without being overwhelmed by the many hurdles they will face.

Through her own initiative, Heather set out to teach her kids how to cook, clean their homes, and pay their bills. She hopes that by extending herself that extra step, she'll help her kids reach for their dreams. Recently, Heather won a $2,000 Unsung Heroes award from the ING Foundation. But she didn't just sit back and bask in her well-deserved praise. Instead, she set her sights on an even bigger award, $25,000, from the same group. With that money, she wants to rent an apartment or house near the school where her kids could acquire useful skills in an onsite, home environment. Heather thinks they'd learn better in a place that would resemble their own future homes or apartments. No one told her to do this. And she's certainly not obligated to spend her prize money helping her students. It's just what she does, a no-brainer.

I've found Heather's positive outlook and dedication in so

many educators. We trust them to care for our kids, and often they go way beyond what we expect of them. We sometimes forget how blessed we are for that. Teachers teach and they protect. Sometimes they risk their lives in the process.

"The art of teaching is the art of assisting discovery."

—Mark Van Doren

Recently, an armed man attacked Rayburn Elementary School in San Antonio. The twenty-six-year-old man first made his way to the library and then to the main office. There, he confronted Shannon Allen, the principal. Though she was only thirty-one years old, and had zero experience with how to handle an armed gunman, she stood her ground when the man threatened her. She was even able to talk him into ditching the gun. Thinking she couldn't see him, he dropped it into a nearby wastebasket.

No one knew exactly what he wanted or why he was in an elementary school. But Shannon just kept talking to him. Soon, he got agitated and moved closer to the wastebasket where he had placed the gun. She tried to keep him away but when he reached for the weapon, she tackled him.

The police arrived and hauled the gunman away.

She saved her kids from what could have been a catastrophe, one that we've unfortunately seen more than once.

"It was pure instinct," Shannon said.

"It all worked out fine," she said, shying away from the limelight.

That's typical of a hero.

I also found another hero in the South Bronx. This neighborhood was literally burning down in the 1980s, devastated by drugs and poverty and government neglect. At one point the city of New York even went so far as to cover many of the broken windows in the abandoned buildings with posters of plants and housecats so passing drivers on the elevated highways wouldn't be distressed at the sight of such dilapidation.

I live only a couple of miles from the Bronx, but my world couldn't seem farther away. That's why I like to go there, because it reminds me of my own youth, of Carvajal Elementary, of those flour tortilla and bean tacos, of the Tower of the Americas. I never want to forget that. Any of it.

I'm sure many kids in the Bronx will remember a great educator named David Banks, who left a career in law to follow another path, that of helping boys. David is man who does not think what he's doing is anything special. It's just what he was meant to do.

Many boys around the country are failing. Or we're failing these boys. I suspect it's the latter. Elementary school–age boys are twice as likely as girls to be diagnosed with learning disabilities, and make up nearly twice the number of girls in special-education classes. By the time they get to college, boys make up only 44 percent of the student body. While that might be great for young men looking for a date, it doesn't indicate much that's good about how we value boys in our culture.

Many educators say it's because boys' brains are wired differently from girls'; therefore boys aren't as interested in learning in today's classroom. But there's another key factor: missing fathers and other mentors. Boys who don't have good male role models in their lives just don't do as well. They flounder. They're like adventurers without a map to guide them.

That's why David founded Eagle Academy, an all-boys' school, where each student is matched with a mentor from the outside. The mentors—all of them—are cops, firefighters, Wall Street big shots, and entrepreneurs. They're regular people demonstrating the heroism in doing what is right and decent.

David grew up the son of a policeman in Queens. His was a close-knit family, providing David with strong role models in his father and uncles. As a result, he and his brothers never got too far out of line. Someone was always there to set them straight. Eventually, he grew up to be a lawyer. But with a bright future ahead of him, he suddenly decided to follow his heart and become an educator instead. Giving up the money, power, and prestige that comes with law to become a teacher is a big deal in this country. He could have pocketed upwards of $500 an hour, but David barely gave it a second thought. He set up Eagle Academy as a charter school. And now he's there every morning at 6 a.m. He chose to teach. And to lead. And to share his vision. He's using his skills to change the world.

"Excellence is to do a common thing
in an uncommon way."

—Booker T. Washington

The Bronx produces many such heroes. Where there's a need, there's a will. Compared to its burnt-down past, the Bronx is booming. Shimon Waronker, an orthodox Jew from Brooklyn, is part of this renaissance.

Junior High School 22 was a place where cops often had to come in to break up fights and riots. On most days, more kids were absent than attending classes. The school went through six principals in just two years. It was hard for the students, most of who were from poor Hispanic and African-American families, to see a future beyond their rough hallways and even rougher streets outside. I instantly related to their plight.

Then Shimon came and took over the school in the fall of 2004. The kids and their parents were shocked to see that Shimon, a member of the Jewish Chabad-Lubavitch branch of Hasidim, wore a beard, a black suit, and a black velvet yarmulke. They'd seen people like him on TV, during the violent riots in the Crown Heights section of Brooklyn that pitted blacks against Jews throughout the 1990s. How could he fit into the neighborhood? Some of the parents would have been less surprised to see him arrive at school in a spaceship—he was that alien to them.

But that's the thing about heroes—they often show up at the most unexpected times, from the most unexpected places. And, in this case, wearing the most unexpected attire.

Shimon worked as a public school teacher for years before joining the first class to graduate from the New York City Leadership Academy, which was founded to help groom future principals. After graduating, he had a tough time getting a job because no one thought he would fit in at most places in the New York City public school system. Most people, however enlightened, would agree.

He was finally hired at Junior High School 22 because no one else wanted the job. No one figured he would last. But he proved them wrong.

Within a couple of years of his arrival, test scores rose, and the school was removed from its former spot on a list of New York City's twelve most dangerous schools. And, amazingly, attendance rose to 93 percent.

Shimon did it by taking huge risks. He fired half the teachers and hired new ones who he felt were better dedicated to their jobs. He listened to these teachers and tried to meet their needs. He paid attention to even minor problems in the hallways and worked especially hard to rid the school of gangs. He went so far as to send some kids to etiquette classes in Manhattan so they would learn proper manners. As Orthodox as he is in his faith, his methods of leading the school were ultra unorthodox.

More impressive than his dedication were his hours. With his wife's blessing, he put a cot in the school where he would sometimes sleep when it was late and he was too tired to travel to Brooklyn, only to come all the way back to school in a few short hours. More important, he communicated with the kids in truly meaningful ways.

Amazingly, Shimon spoke Spanish. Because he grew up in Chile, and did not learn English until he arrived in the U.S. at age eleven, he was able to bring into the school parents who were leery of the system so they could learn to be a part of their children's future. He was the most unlikely sort of Latino any kid from the South Bronx could imagine.

For him, it's just part of being a citizen of the world. Shimon believes that God put him on earth to make things better. The school's shared goal (students, teachers, and parents), he says, is to help the kids dream.

This is the example we need. Shimon isn't doing anything any other dedicated principal couldn't do. He's not Superman. The difference is that he follows his heart. He believes in his kids, his school, and in himself, and he's not afraid to take risks to fulfill his personal duty. His neighbors back in Brooklyn wonder why he's not helping "his own." Even the people he's helping wonder why he's there. But for Shimon it's only natural. He believes we're all connected. You help one person and you're helping everyone else. And in the process, you get a lift from knowing you can actually make a difference.

I remember how valuable some of my teachers were to me. Seeing Shimon and David helping kids from neighborhoods considered lost causes makes me feel good about our country. America is full of heroes. And our culture has the potential to create many more. If only more people had such vision and acted upon it. When we strive for a larger purpose, it affects everyone for the better.

Ordinary People, Extraordinary Choices
You Make the Call!

The cocktail party is rolling along with lots of great conversations. You don't know many people here, but you're enjoying yourself immensely until a respectable-looking woman in a beautiful black dress starts talking to you about her housekeeper. Apparently, the housekeeper is from Brazil. And she's not doing a very good job.

"You know, she's very dark," says the woman, nodding knowingly. "I thought that alone would make her a good housekeeper, but I guess that whole Brazilian Latin thing just makes her lazy."

You don't know that much about Brazil, and you don't even have a housekeeper, but her remarks immediately make you very uncomfortable.

YOU COULD:

A) Nod knowingly, wanting to keep this wealthy woman's favor.

B) Excuse yourself by saying you need to refresh your drink.

C) Accidentally on purpose step on her open-toed wedgies with your sharp-toed high heels and push down a bit too long before saying, "Oh, excuse me."

D) Ask her to please refrain from making generalizations about people based on their skin color and national origin because you find it offensive.

Racism is one of the most insidious cancers in American society—and in other countries around the world. And I think that anything we can do to stop it is worth the effort—as long as it's a sensible action, of course. Many people are made so uncomfortable by expressions of racism that they resort to answer A. Having been a recipient of biased remarks myself, I can't accept that A is right. B is no better. The passive-aggressiveness of C probably wouldn't get your message across very clearly. But D sounds good to me: you can't control her, but you can sure let her know how you feel.

Ordinary People, Extraordinary Choices
You Make the Call!

It's the week for standardized state exams, and you've got plenty of them. The studying is getting to you so you start goofing around looking at web-sites. One site leads you to some classified ads geared toward high school kids in your neighborhood. There you see an ad offering answers to the up-coming biology exam that you just spent three grueling hours preparing for. You think your teacher would be devastated to see this. But you sure wouldn't mind knowing in advance the answers to all the questions. You think you know the kid who is selling this easy route to a perfect score.

YOU COULD:

A) Pay the 20 dollars and get a copy of all the answers.

B) Surf away from the ad and pretend it never happened.

C) Call the kid and tell him to take the ad down.

D) Tell your teacher, in confidence, what you've found.

This is a tough one. No one wants to be a rat. But if some people buy the test results in advance, they'll have an unfair advantage over all the kids who don't. That will skew the test scores and could lead to all sorts of problems for a lot of people. So while answer A might seem like a harm-less purchase, it won't be. Neither would B. Closing your eyes to the problem won't make it any better for anyone but you. I don't think option C would accomplish much but give you a bad reputation. So I'd definitely go with D: you're taking the risk of being called a rat, but you'll be help-ing a lot of people in the long run.

CHAPTER THREE

What Makes a Hero?

W e're in the midst of a bad case of hero confusion. Sometimes it seems as if we worship people who haven't done much with their lives besides make themselves famous or rich or both. Entire magazines are devoted to fatuousness. Generally, the only heroes you read about are the ones who make the big plays.

The opposite is also true. There's a tendency these days to label everyone from the person who picks up after his dog to the mail carrier who arrives on time as a hero. The everyday heroes who take big risks get lost in the shuffle. It happens a lot these days. But these special people deserve more.

There are plenty of ordinary folks doing extraordinary things. In fact, today heroes are more likely to have committed small acts of kindness and selflessness. In many cases, the larger heroes of the past have failed us in the present.

There's a fascinating book titled *The Hero, American Style*, by a historian named Marshall Fishwick. In it, he analyzes the different types of heroes Americans are drawn to. And he makes this insightful observation: "The hero is always a barometer to the national climate of opinion. Every hero mirrors the time and place in which he lives. He must reflect men's innermost hopes and beliefs in a public way."

Today, that reflection is not of amazing leaders and far-thinking businesspeople. There are few billionaires doing great works these days—although I want to give a loud shout-out to Bill Gates and his efforts to improve the lives of millions through disease prevention and improved schooling. But the reflection we see now is of everyday heroes. Having "smaller" heroes—people that you and I can relate to in a true way—is not a bad thing. It's a good thing. A sign of how well our culture adapts.

We live in a time where huge institutions have lost their center. The government seems out of control. Our wars seem endless. The corporations we once relied on for stability and a safe avenue into the future now change names and services in a heartbeat. Institutional loyalty seems like a thing from a fairy tale.

While we can still look to the great heroes of our past, such as Martin Luther King Jr. or Florence Nightingale, for inspiration, more and more these days our heroes aren't grand figures. They're our neighbors, our family members, and our friends. Our heroes are the magnanimous strangers who help us. They are the soldiers and police officers who struggle every day to defend us. They're the firefighters who never quit. They're the teachers who wake up every morning and step into the day with the hope that they can change their students' lives. They're the accountants, IT managers, warehouse fork-lift operators, checkout clerks, ditch diggers, ticket takers, plumbers, and bank tellers who put their lives on the line each day so that another person might live.

"Continuous effort—not strength or intelligence—is the key to unlocking our potential."

—Winston Churchill

Every year the Carnegie Hero Fund Commission honors dozens of people who risked their lives trying to save someone else. Often the rescuer and the rescued are total strangers. It's fitting that the Carnegie Foundation gives these awards. The foundation's original benefactor, the Scottish robber baron Andrew Carnegie, established his bona fides as a hero by having libraries built in towns across the English-speaking world back in the late nineteenth century. In his life, Carnegie gave away about $350 million, much of which is still at work.

Carnegie set up the Hero Fund in 1904 following a huge coal-mine explosion in Pennsylvania that killed 181 people. Two of those killed had gone back into the mine to rescue the others. Their heroism inspired Carnegie to offer a $5 million endowment so the fund could honor heroes and help the families of those who are killed or left disabled because of their heroism. The award includes the Carnegie Medal, grants, scholarships, and other aid as needed. Over more than a hundred years, the fund has given out over nine thousand medals.

Curiously, most of the Carnegie fund heroes have been men. Fewer than 10 percent have been women. I think that's because so many of the Carnegie heroes are people who've had great physical abilities that allowed them to run into burning buildings or dive into raging rivers to rescue another person. But from my experience, women are probably more inclined toward heroism than men.

My first hero, of course, was my mother. And in my life as a reporter, roving the world in some of the most difficult situations imaginable, I've found that women are more likely to put their lives, reputations, and finances on the line to help others. They just don't seem as worried about the possible negative consequences when given the chance to help another person.

***

Louann Brizendine, MD, has written a fascinating book titled *The Female Brain,* and—watch out men—she's writing another called *The Male Brain*. As a psychiatrist at the University of California, San Francisco, she's spent a lot of time looking into the brain chemistry behind our personalities.

According to Dr. Brizendine, there are different systems at work in the brain. One uses dopamine as the neurotransmitter and is responsible for our instantaneous responses. You could call it the teenage brain because it bypasses all the areas of our minds that worry about consequences. This system helps some people to respond heroically to emergencies without worrying about the dangers.

"You jump in the water and save the drowning child," said Dr. Brizendine. "There's no time to go through what we call the thinking, or frontal cortex."

Instead, these signals go through the nucleus accumbens areas of the brain. When dopamine surges happen here, the brain is put on high alert.

"It says 'pay attention immediately to this,'" said Dr. Brizendine. "It pulls the alarm in a way that goes straight to muscle action, rather than going through the thinking part of the brain, the frontal cortex, where we plan things, decide whether something will be good or bad for you, or assess the consequences of our actions."

When a person does something heroic, it is going through this part of the brain. In a way, heroes are like teenagers. We are amazed at the risks they take and the way they disregard their own safety. We judge them with our frontal cortex.

But not everyone has a highly developed ability to bypass his or her frontal cortex—meaning not everyone is a hero. And that's a good thing. The world would be crazier than it is if everyone engaged in risky heroics. Heroes have a special setup that allows their brains to bypass processes that make most of us cautious. According to Dr. Brizendine, it's normal to be cautious. It is not normal to be a hero, although in special circumstances, all of us can bypass the cautious side of our brains.

"I remember walking down the beach near the Golden Gate Bridge with my two-and-a-half-year-old son when a big wave came up and took him out. I was wearing a down jacket, but I ran out and grabbed the top of his hair under the water and pulled him out. I didn't think about it. But later, when my frontal cortex started working on it, I freaked out and was scared to death," said Dr. Brizendine.

As soon as a hero starts to react to a crisis, adrenaline starts flowing through the body, giving the seemingly superhuman strength that is said to let people lift cars off injured children, or pull debris off someone trapped in a building collapse. This adrenaline rush shuts down your immune system, along with other systems in your body, so you wouldn't want to have it happening all the time. But it lets you focus on the task at hand.

This often happens in driving situations. You see something stupid—like a person pulls out in front of you—and you just react to avoid it. But afterward your heart rate goes up. We've all felt it.

Some people are more prone to heroics than others. Every population has to have different types of people in order to survive. Cautious people survive better than others in areas where there aren't many emergencies. Heroes do better where there is stress. But if everyone had heroic personalities, and the accompanying tendencies to be more assertive and aggressive, they might not do so well in peaceful locations. Every society needs thoughtful, methodical people to be judges, lawyers, and leaders. There's less of a need for lots of heroes. But we do need a few.

"I would speculate that one to five percent of people are natural heroes. They are born that way," said Dr. Brizendine.

Today, neuroscientists believe that temperament is a matter of genetics—you're born with your personality. Of course, your environment and your experiences growing up—whether you were nurtured or abandoned, whether you had opportunities or not—can make a natural hero more inclined toward heroism. And it can make some who are not naturally inclined toward heroism act that way when needed.

These latter people are accidental heroes, says Dr. Brizendine, and she estimates that they make up 20 percent of the population. When they find themselves in the right place at a certain time, they seize the opportunity to do the right thing.

But the thing about heroic behavior is that it's out of the ordinary. The challenge for us, I think, is to make good works and good deeds a commonplace part of our lives. If we do that, heroism will spread. It can start with small things, such as offering your seat on the bus to a pregnant woman. Anything that becomes an expected behavior will increase exponentially.

E. Scott Geller, alumni distinguished professor of psychology at Virginia Tech University, has studied behavior for years. He believes there are three main components to heroism: competence, commitment, and courage. And the one factor that makes those three come together is compassion.

"Hitler had courage, but he had no compassion," said Dr. Geller.

According to Dr. Geller, we can't hide from the fact that some people have natural tendencies toward heroism, just as some people are shyer than other people. But he believes anyone can overcome these limitations and develop heroic traits. People can train each other to be caring and supportive of others, he said.

"This is what this society needs," he added. "We need people stepping to the plate and thinking about others. It's as simple as asking strangers in a van to buckle up, to helping your neighbor carry groceries into the house. As a culture, we need these purposeful acts of kindness. And as we practice them, they'll grow."

"The welfare of each is bound up in the welfare of all."

—Helen Keller

Stanford professor Philip Zimbardo has written a fascinating book, *The Lucifer Effect*, about how lab experiments he conducted show the capacity even good people have to do "bad" things. He's discovered that when regular people are put in unfamiliar situations, with unfamiliar pressures on them, they can often be easily manipulated into doing evil in ways that they normally wouldn't think of. His work suggests that our nature is not the sole factor determining how good or evil we turn out to be.

The same things that make it easy for some people to become evil also allow them to be heroes. Dr. Zimbardo's research shows that humans can choose kindness over indifference, and be heroes rather than villains. It's a choice that can be taught. He says that we need to teach children to be "heroes in waiting," who will be prepared to do the right thing if, sometime in their life, they find themselves in the situation where they could choose to be a hero.

According to Dr. Zimbardo, while most people will follow the crowd into evil behavior, there is always that person who will refuse to participate. These people are heroes. And most of them will deny that they are in any way heroic.

Dr. Zimbardo believes we can all work on building our "heroic imagination" by imagining difficult situations and hypothetical problems and figuring out the best way to act. Imagine, for instance, what you might do if you came across someone making a sexist remark to a store clerk. Would you say something or let it pass? Imagining the right response is a good way to train yourself to respond well if the situation ever arises in real life. The more you imagine, the stronger your hero response will become. Envision yourself as capable of being a hero and that's what you will become.

Ordinary People, Extraordinary Choices
You Make the Call!

Early on a Saturday morning you roll out of bed to go for a jog. It's your special time, when you connect with nature and kick out all the kinks from the previous week before starting to enjoy the weekend. As you step out the door you hear the approaching sanitation truck on the weekly recycling run. All the neighbors have their blue bins full of glass and plastic and green bins full of paper at curbside. You're surprised to see the old guy from down the street dragging a tub of mixed trash to the curb—but instead of putting it in front of his own house, he sticks it in front of his next-door neighbor's. The sanitation dudes will never pick it up. And surely that house will get a $100 fine for violating the recycling rules.

YOU COULD:

A) Pretend you didn't see anything and get on with your peaceful jog.

B) Run past the old guy and give him your nastiest look.

C) Wait till he goes back inside and then drag the can over to his driveway.

D) Run up to him and say that you'd appreciate it if he didn't do that kind of thing, because it only hurts an innocent person.

Surprisingly, this kind of thing happens pretty often. In my New York neighborhood it's not uncommon for people to dump their trash in other people's areas, just to avoid having the responsibility of dealing with it themselves. Clearly, the old guy is in the wrong. And if you follow A, you can definitely kiss being a hero goodbye. Giving the old guy a nasty look won't do too much good either—passive-aggressive behavior like that usually just creates tension. C is an attractive choice, because you seemingly solve the problem without any confrontation. But in my book, D is the heroic choice: You're taking a risk in approaching the man, but it's a risk that should be taken.

CHAPTER FOUR

Never Too Young to Be a Hero

When I was a kid, my world was pretty safe. Thanks to my mom and dad, no matter what perils surrounded me in the old neighborhood, I always felt protected. My mom made sure I was at home most of the time. It was her way of trying to keep me out of harm's way. And it worked. I didn't have my first drink until I was eighteen years old. And I've never smoked a cigarette. My mother's voice still rings in my head whenever I think about doing something she wouldn't have approved of.

Yet, however strict my mother may have been, she knew that at some point she had to let me go. All parents have to deal with this crossroads; knowing when to let your children spread their wings is one of those moments a parent never forgets. Most of us can only hope we've given them the tools to determine right from wrong when it really counts.

Fortunately, kids are incredibly resilient and they often

have fantastic instincts. I'm always impressed and relieved when I come across one of these young heroes. Each has inspired in me the hope that my own children would act in kind.

One of the most amazing stories I've encountered took place during the aftermath of Hurricane Katrina, when large portions of New Orleans lay completely underwater. Most of us saw the aftermath of Katrina play out on our television screens in the comfort of our living rooms. It was hard to believe what was happening. And yet, when all the amazing stories of what everyone went through came to light in the months that followed the devastation, there was one I just couldn't shake.

"You gain strength, courage and confidence by every experience in which you really stop to look fear in the face. . . . You must do the thing you think you cannot do."

—Eleanor Roosevelt

Looking out the second-story window, De'Monte Love and his family saw people floating by on mattresses and sofas. It had been two days since Hurricane Katrina had devastated New Orleans, and six-year-old De'Monte was itching to go outside. His stomach hurt from hunger and it was hot.

After waiting for what seemed like an eternity, De'Monte's mother, Catrina (the name is an eerie coincidence), and his aunt, Felecia, decided to try to flag down one of the helicopters flying overhead. They hoped it would rescue them. When one passed low enough, De'Monte's mother leaned out the window with her youngest baby, Da'Roneal, to get the pilot's attention. The pilot motioned that the family should go up to the roof of their house. Along with a few neighbors, De'Monte's family crowded onto a third-floor balcony, just below the roof, as the helicopter landed. A few people were already up on the roof talking with the pilot. Everyone was shocked when the pilot told them he could only take the children. All the adults had to stay behind. The mothers protested. What mother wouldn't?

"He'll come back for you," said one of the male neighbors who had talked with the pilot.

The mothers continued to resist. They didn't want to give their children to strangers. After what they had gone through in the previous forty-eight hours, their suspicion had grown to the point where everything seemed like a potential danger. On the other hand, each mother wanted to save her child. No one knew how many more days they would spend trapped in the incredible heat without food or water.

The neighbors finally persuaded the mothers that this was a matter of life and death and there was no other option. It could literally be a once-in-a-lifetime chance. The pilot told the group he would take the children to a place called Overleaf, Texas. Overleaf. That sounded nice, the women thought, and shady; a good place, and far from their flooded and destroyed neighborhood.

Felecia lifted her baby Ty're and gave him to the men on the roof to hand over to the waiting helicopter pilot. Next up was two-year-old Zarione. As one of the neighbors took her, both mother and daughter burst into tears.

Catrina handed up her four-month-old Da'Roneal to the men waiting on the roof. She then handed up six-year-old De'Monte. Another mother passed up two-year-old Leewood and two-year-old Gabrielle.

Six kids in all joined De'Monte on that helicopter. He was the oldest. De'Monte was the only one who knew enough, or so the mothers thought at the time, to guide them back to their families. The others were far too young to communicate effectively.

Just before the helicopter was set to take off, another woman from their building scaled the roof and begged the pilot to take her. She had two children, one of whom had severe disabilities, and she said he wouldn't be able to make it on his own. The chopper was almost full, but he could see the truth in her plea. The pilot relented.

As the helicopter rose into the sky, the women fell together sobbing.

"I was scared and I didn't know what to do," De'Monte said later. "I thought I wouldn't see my mom again."

When the helicopter dropped the kids off on a grassy me-

dian just off Interstate 10, De'Monte took it upon himself to
guide his little brother, two cousins, and three other kids he
didn't really know, through whatever lay ahead.

✳

When De'Monte's story hit the news, it was sensationalized
into a tale of one young boy performing an almost impossible
task: caring for six young children, some of them in diapers,
all by himself for several days as he shepherded them around
a chaos-stricken Louisiana, and all the way to San Antonio.
Just a little boy with a big heart and limitless courage. There's
an iconic photo of De'Monte: a six-year-old boy carrying a
five-month-old. He's walking down a flood-ravaged road, surrounded by five determined toddlers. The image will stay with
me forever.

But the truth, as first described in *Waters Dark and Deep*
by Katie Thomas, while less implausible is equally dramatic.
De'Monte is still the true hero of this story, but he wouldn't
have made it through with his young charges without the help
of many other people who formed a long chain of heroes.

The first link in the chain were the helicopter pilots who
risked so much to land on rooftops and rescue flood victims
across all of New Orleans. Second, the mother on the chopper
who pleaded to be let on and who, when they landed, asked a
U.S. Army major to look out for De'Monte and the toddlers
while she cared for her own two kids.

The Army major did as the mother instructed and watched

over the brood as the hours passed, and the sun-beaten grass turned to a mud-caked field of fetid garbage. Finally, in the late afternoon, two paramedics loaded the kids into their ambulance for the long ride to Baton Rouge. The kids slept most of the way. When they pulled into the emergency staging area at Jimmy Swaggart Ministries, Department of Health workers met them and took them to an emergency shelter set up specifically for children.

De'Monte kept a wary eye on the other kids as the relief workers helped them shower, eat, and change into fresh clothes.

Meanwhile, Catrina, Felecia, and the other mothers waited in vain for the helicopter to return. Catrina took comfort in the fact that she'd taught De'Monte their phone number, address, and full name. She knew he'd take care of business. That's just the kind of kid he was. But she couldn't help but worry as five more hours passed before another helicopter was able to rescue them.

"Where are my kids?" she asked the chopper pilots.

They had no idea. They'd also never heard of Overleaf, Texas. It turned out that no one had. The place didn't exist. What the pilot had actually said must've been lost amid all the emotion and confusion. The mothers who had freely given their kids to those on the helicopter had no idea where their kids might be. They felt dread as the chopper dropped them off at an airport near Lake Pontchartrain.

Felecia and Catrina ran through the crowds frantically

looking for their kids. But nobody could tell them anything. No one could help at all. They begged for information. Someone told them people were being sent to Dallas. Another said Baton Rouge. Another said Houston. San Antonio. Biloxi. And on and on. But not a single person had ever heard of Overleaf, Texas.

They passed that night sleeping on top of boxes of bottled water in the open air. Then they were herded aboard another helicopter that they hoped would take them to Texas, and their children. Instead, it landed after just a few minutes at another airport on the far side of town. As they exited, they were hit by the stench of human sweat and waste as a mass of lost people drifted about in the sea of trash.

Then they were told to board a plane. They continued asking for their children. No one knew anything about them. Amazingly, in that huge crowd, they finally ran into one of the officials who had helped De'Monte and the others. The official assured them that their children were safe in Baton Rouge. The news brought just enough relief for them to make it through the day. But worry wouldn't abate until each mother could hold her child.

Next, they were told they couldn't go to Baton Rouge, even if their kids were there—they had to go somewhere else. So they boarded a plane for San Antonio. They were told they'd be reunited with De'Monte and the others when all the initial confusion settled down. The flight that carried Catrina and Felecia to San Antonio was their first time ever on a plane.

Even though they'd just been on a helicopter the day before, that flight was almost as terrifying to them as the hurricane.

Back at the shelter in Baton Rouge, De'Monte, who had just started first grade, began to let details of what had happened to him out for the first time: the flood, the helicopter, his father and mother's phone number.

As you might expect, the shelter workers were a little suspicious of information De'Monte began relaying, especially after he said his mother was named Catrina. After all, that was the name of the hurricane that had just ripped their world apart and, surely, the boy was dealing with psychological trauma. But De'Monte persisted. He kept his eye on all four toddlers, one of whom wore nothing but a diaper, as they drifted to sleep that night on emergency cots. The next day, more children arrived. Then more. But De'Monte and the others stuck together. Days passed.

On Friday, four days after the hurricane struck, Catrina and her sister, Felecia, were flown into San Antonio. Houston already had 15,000 evacuees and the government had decided to make San Antonio the next large-scale evacuation center. I can understand why, having reported from the Astrodome during that horrible disaster. No one would have wanted to stay there.

At the shelter, someone took photos of the kids, and sent those, along with any biographical information they could get, to the National Center for Missing and Exploited Children. This heroic organization is the group behind the Amber

Alerts, and it has many volunteers around the country. One special response team from the NCMEC is called Team Adam, and it's composed of highly qualified people, many of them retired police, who will drop what they are doing in an instant when there are missing children in need.

While the photos of De'Monte and the others were being collected and sent, Felecia was in San Antonio talking to the people at the missing person's table in her shelter, which was run by the Texas Department of Child Protective Services. Her sister, Catrina, had been taken to the hospital with complications from diabetes and she was resting there. At the missing person's desk, a volunteer ex-police officer from Team Adam listened to Felecia and the others. They took down as much information as they could.

By the next day, Catrina had returned and the mothers were interviewed again by an officer from Team Adam. He decided to make this case—the seven missing children guided by six-year-old De'Monte Love—his top priority. He made sure the home office, in Washington, D.C., kept a lookout for the kids' parents.

Almost immediately, they made a match. A woman in San Antonio was looking for her daughter Gabrielle. And the shelter in Baton Rouge had put out a search for the mother of a little girl named Gabby. But finding Gabrielle's mother among the twenty-five hundred evacuees already sheltered in San Antonio was like looking for a needle in a haystack. She'd left the missing person's office to return to wherever, among those thousands of people, she'd set up camp. There was no public address system and very little organization, so the volunteers did it the old-fashioned way. They hand-lettered a sign with Gabrielle's mother's name on it and walked around with it. Within a half hour, they had found her.

They contacted Angel Flight, a brave group of volunteer pilots who use their own planes to fly charity missions. The group agreed to fly the children up from Baton Rouge to be with their mothers. Word got out and the media descended on Baton Rouge, where De'Monte served as the kids' spokesperson. They took baths, put on fresh clothes, and boarded the plane.

At the airport in San Antonio, the mothers were shocked to find a phalanx of TV cameras and reporters. The kids climbed into their mothers' arms and didn't let go. De'Monte, the true hero, lit up the newscasts that night and his story was splashed in newspapers and magazines the next day. The youngest hero, they called him. And they were right.

De'Monte was thrust into his courageous role, and did an amazing job. His story gave people hope that they too would be reunited with their lost loved ones. And in times like that, when disaster strikes and one is witness to the worst, hope is priceless.

I'm still amazed that those mothers were able to keep their sanity after having to make the incredibly painful—yet correct, in my view—decision to put their kids in the hands of strangers to be flown in a helicopter across the flood-ravaged city to God knew where. The floodwaters were up to their building's second story. They had little food left, and what they did have was rapidly spoiling. There was no clean water, nowhere to get diapers. The kids were getting sick. It really says something about how far, mentally and physically, parents will go to keep their children safe. They did the right thing.

And yet, there were detractors. Many people criticized these women. "How could they leave a child like that?" "How could any mother abandon her baby?" But they miss the point. These women were abandoning their egos to save their babies. And that takes incredible courage.

Everyone who helped these mothers and De'Monte and the countless others were filled with this same courage. The national guardsmen, ambulance drivers, and shelter volunteers. The air rescue operation that delivered Catrina and Felecia to San Antonio. The health workers. The cooks. The volunteers. The millions of people who donated goods and money to help the hurricane victims. Hurricane Katrina brought out the hero in so many people. And little De'Monte was the innocent face of it all.

Unlike De'Monte, who was unwillingly thrust into his heroic role, others purposefully seek to do whatever they can to right the wrongs of the world. Andreina Cordova is one of these people.

"Nothing liberates our greatness like the desire to help."

—Marianne Williamson

Andreina Cordova was a smart Los Angeles teen who risked her own reputation to help other teens avoid some of the pitfalls she had witnessed on the road to becoming an adult. She started talking to her peers about sex and its consequences; how a little knowledge can go a long way toward keeping a person safe and on the right track.

Sounds straightforward enough. But imagine the giggles in the hallways of her school when kids heard she wanted to talk to them about, well, the perilous world of, giggle-giggle, *that*.

When she was fourteen, Andreina became a "peer advocate" with Planned Parenthood's Ujima Program. Ujima means "working together" in Swahili, which is the official language of four East African nations. The goal of the Ujima Program is to help kids receive correct information about sexual health and pregnancy, while learning responsible behavior patterns, such as contraception and abstinence. This may not be necessary in all high schools, but where Andreina grew up this knowledge was vitally important. Andreina's neighborhood, South Central Los Angeles, has one of the highest teen pregnancy rates in the nation. She had seen so many of the young people she knew make poor decisions that altered the rest of their lives. She wanted to do what she could to save a few from going down that road.

Andreina first got interested in the issue in middle school, when she was surprised to hear kids gossiping about other kids who were having sex. The sex talk took her off guard, and she almost didn't believe it until a girl she knew got pregnant and disappeared from school. This left an indelible mark on her.

So when Andreina, who is the fifth of five girls in her family, heard that Planned Parenthood taught kids to help other kids, she signed up, becoming one of the youngest ever to become a peer advocate for the organization. No matter what people have against Planned Parenthood, and there are many who do have strong opinions about the organization, I'm glad it exists to help those in need of answers and to empower young girls like Andreina to help spread solid, factual information about health. This matters. Andreina is living proof of that.

The organization taught her how to lead workshops called "Healthy Love" at her school. And Andreina promotes safe sex everywhere, from bus stops to malls—wherever teenagers congregate. You can usually find her talking to kids after school as they head out the doors to soccer practice or home. Many may consider Andreina's tactics a nuisance, or an invasion of privacy. But to her, she's making kids aware. She knows that her peers do more than they would ever admit to when confronted by a parent or a teacher. Andreina helps to bridge this gap with her enthusiasm and her ability to memorize statistics.

She's read tons of books, and memorized most of the stats about Los Angeles County, such as that every year 360,000 kids who are infected with a sexually transmitted disease and more than five thousand girls under eighteen give birth.

South Los Angeles, where Andreina lives, has the highest rate of teen births and teen STDs in the county. She has no trouble speaking frankly. And for the most part, the kids listen.

Boys tend to squirm a little more than girls when Andreina talks about sex. But some of them come to her later, in confidence, with questions. She helps them. One could just imagine the trouble she has surely helped many teenagers avoid. I find her openness and bravery to be true heroism.

Patrick Kohlman is educating kids in another way, about a very personal situation, but one that sets him right up on par with Andreina. Patrick's a great example of how, sometimes, when a youngster simply stands up for himself he becomes an inspiration to others. Patrick is a thirteen-year-old from Islip, New York.

He isn't the biggest kid around, and he doesn't come across as someone who is unusually brave. Middle school wasn't easy for him. He was one of those children that other kids pick on. And even assault.

Patrick was assaulted in and out of school more often than he wants to recall. One day a bully told him he would kill him the next day. This prompted his worried parents to talk with the school officials. Nothing was done. The bully beat Patrick over the head with a rock. The physical wounds healed but the psychological scar was devastating.

The harassment and threats continued. Finally, Patrick grew tired of it all and started fighting back. This got him into more trouble, even though he believed he had a right to defend himself.

He realized he couldn't keep fighting everyone. And he knew there would always be someone bigger than him who wanted to do him harm. Struggling to find a way to deal with the problem, he decided he wanted to give a speech to the teachers at his school about what he'd gone through. But it was near the end of his seventh-grade year and there was no time in the school schedule. So he got the wild idea to make a video about bullying to show at the next PTA meeting. He spent a month working on the video, doing research on the Web, tracking down photos, and setting the whole thing to music. The resulting video, called "Through My Eyes," is a moving series of photos and images that highlight the fear that victims of bullying feel on a daily basis. There's an image of a boy on a school bus with three larger kids sitting menacingly behind him, as well as a photo of a woman who was actually slashed across her face four times with a knife. The video is incredibly powerful.

Some of the frames include Patrick's thoughts on bullying, such as "I have gone to the school before for help, yet the violence got worse. . . . Now I am here telling you what is going on . . . asking you for help. . . . Not only for me, but for all the people out there who are being bullied."

When the principal of his school wouldn't let him show the

video because he felt the images were too graphic, Patrick decided to post it on YouTube, the video-sharing service on the Internet.

Since then, more than a hundred thousand people have seen it, and thousands have posted comments on the site. Most are along these lines:

> *AWESOME JOB PATRICK! Let's hope the schools and the bullies will watch and listen. Just remember to keep staying strong, keep standing up and fighting for your rights! I am proud of you for standing up to these bullies, your school should be ashamed of itself. YOU ROCK!*

A number of newspapers have written about Patrick. I first came across him in a video report playing in the backseat of my NYC taxi. What a hero, I thought. His video generated a lot of publicity, which is exactly what he hoped for. That fame has helped many kids feel less lonely about being bullied. While the video didn't immediately solve Patrick's problems, it sure helped others become aware that a problem existed. And there's nothing like being a celebrity to improve your profile at school. Patrick offers a great lesson on how taking a stance about your own bad situation and doing whatever you can to make it better can have a ripple effect on the lives of countless others.

Brianna Vogel, of Austin, Texas, definitely understands the ripple effect. She started doing some remarkable stuff when she was just five years old. Brianna's brother, Devon, suffered common variable immune deficiency, a rare disease that ravaged his immune system. When she visited him on the pediatric ward, they got bored because there wasn't much for them to play with. She got the idea to raise money to buy arts and crafts supplies to give all the kids in the hospital, as well as their visitors, something to do.

Brianna started by collecting pennies from friends and family. And she told people to make donations instead of giving her birthday presents. She then came up with an ingenious idea to find a hundred people who would raise $125 each to give to her cause. She hoped that would be enough money to help other children's wards, too. By the time she was eight, Brianna had set up a nonprofit foundation called Brianna's Pennies of Love. So far, she's raised thousands of dollars to buy art supplies for kids in hospitals. Her foundation continues to grow and she even gives lectures around Austin, at churches and business, explaining her cause. She's an example to many.

※

Kyla Olvera is another example of how so many young kids truly shine. She was a typical five-year-old who loved to play with dolls, draw pictures, and hang out with her babysitter when her mother was away from their home near Lake Mead, Nevada. One day she was playing with her babysitter (who was pregnant) and her one-year-old sister, when the babysitter collapsed and passed out.

"Everything went numb and I hit the floor," the babysitter recalled. "I don't know what happened."

Kyla immediate called 911.

"I told them that she plugged in the vacuum and then fell to the floor," said Kyla.

She never cried. And she took care of her one-year-old sister until the paramedics arrived.

She claims she's not a hero. But I know better.

These five-year-olds can really surprise you. They certainly amaze me. When I hear stories about them, such as Brianna's or Kyla's, I can't help but think, was I ever capable of conducting myself the way they did, when the time came? It's a thought-provoking question for all of us.

Sometimes kids become heroes in the more traditional way, by risking their lives to save others. That happened to four eighth-grade Las Vegas boys not too long ago. DeShon Polk, Sylvester St. Cyr, Fernando Chavez, and Brent Stockhausen regularly took the school bus home together. One afternoon their bus slowed down to make a turn and a pickup truck slammed into it from behind. The truck's engine caught fire and the flames jumped onto the back of the bus. As the bus burned, the bus driver struggled to get the front door open. But to no avail. That's when Polk and St. Cyr ordered the other kids to use the emergency exit in the middle of the bus. But first, the two boys had to kick it open, because it was also stuck.

The boys helped all the kids off the bus. Stockhausen even had to catch a couple of girls as they jumped out the window. When they noticed an oily puddle forming underneath the truck the kids started to panic, fearing it might explode.

Stockhausen and Chavez ran to a church and got a fire extinguisher. By the time they returned, the fire was too big to put out, so they waited a few more minutes for the fire department. Police and fire crews soon arrived and put out the blaze. One kid had to go to the hospital but no other kids were seriously hurt. The boys deny they are brave, but I insist they are. It's this can-do, selfless spirit of giving that line the hearts of heroes everywhere.

Sometimes it's easy to look around the mall, or read the magazines, and start to feel hopeless about the state of young America. Too materialistic. Not interested enough in books and reading, or too consumed by text messaging and computer profiles. Do they really want to help anyone but themselves? But then I come across one of these stories and I feel better. Reassured.

Ordinary People, Extraordinary Choices
You Make the Call!

The walk to school has always been pleasant for you, and the flowers and trees along the way put you in a good mood for class. But this day you hear shouting going on as you turn the corner towards the playground. You can't believe it: one of the football players has cornered another kid and is taunting him with chants of "Death to Goths." The kid looks terrified behind his purple bangs. Now you've never been that much into the Goth habit of wearing black clothes and listening to depressing music, but neither do you like to see people tormented. As you get near, one of the football player's buddies sees you staring and tells you to get lost.

YOU COULD:

A) Turn the other way and walk into school.

B) Insist that the bullies stop what they're doing.

C) Dive in and start swinging your fists.

D) Look for a teacher to help you out.

I remember scenes like this from my own school days, and to tell you the truth, I'd often just keep walking out of fear of antagonizing one of the gangsters in our neighborhood. I'm not proud of that, but I think we're all aware of the role fear plays in heroics. But A isn't the only answer if you're afraid of getting hurt. D is the best option here. B might work, but it might get you into trouble. And C would just be taking too much of a gamble, if the Goth wasn't facing a serious physical threat.

CHAPTER FIVE

The Nurturing Tribe

W here would we be without our families?

It's a question many of us are forced to ponder when we find ourselves in the middle of a long run of bad luck. Who else but our families is there for us, no matter what?

And then there are certain peculiarities that also come with family.

There's a great quote from the comedian Martin Mull about the crazy situations we get ourselves into in the age-old quest to be part of a tribe: "A family is like having a bowling alley installed inside your brain."

As much as I love my family, I can certainly relate.

It's true that daily life, with kids, a spouse, parents and grandparents, uncles and aunts, can be a frustratingly chaotic experience. It's a given that family provides life with thousands of examples of beauty, but it also comes with plenty of hard times and tragedy. And just when it all seems too over-whelming, that moment arrives when someone in your family steps up and takes a risk. For those few moments, everyone works together. The ball rolls purposefully down its lane and into a solid strike, and you realize it's nice to have that bowling alley in your brain.

In the end, I believe that heroes are grown and nurtured by their families. A hero's training ground would be incomplete without the turmoil, without the pressure, and surely without the support and love a family provides.

I found a great example of this in my hometown.

Louis Barrios, Diana Barrios-Trevino, and Teresa Barrios-Ogden are three remarkable siblings from San Antonio who personify the way family bonds can lead to heroic acts. The family owns two Mexican restaurants in San Antonio that are legendary for their "puffy tacos"—fresh masa dough deep-fried to form wonderfully airy tacos that draw people from all over the world. They really are that good. For decades, visitors to Los Barrios's restaurants got an added treat in Viola Barrios, the matriarch and founder of the family business. Viola greeted every customer with a warm smile. She bestowed the kindness the Barrioses are known for onto everyone. This made what happened to the family, to Viola, even more shocking.

San Antonio can be a rough place. Witness this lineup of stories that recently aired on a single night on one local TV news broadcast:

- Drive-by Shooting & Crash Victim Dies
- Murder Suspect Leads Police to Victim
- Shooting Ends with Crash
- Major Busts along the Border
- Burglary Victim Gets Shot with His Own Rifle
- Homeless Man Starts Fire in Vacant Home
- Man Starts Fire at Auto Parts Store
- Outspoken Civil Rights Attorney Pleads Guilty to Crime
- Officer Involved in Shooting
- Teacher Facing Drug, Handgun Charges

Clearly, violence is nothing new in the land of puffy tacos. But nobody could have anticipated the gruesome fate that befell seventy-six-year-old Viola Barrios one spring evening in 2008. Most people thought a flock of angels watched over her, given what she had done for her community, as well as the way she struggled for years as a single mom to make sure that with her singular humility and determination her kids were well fed, well educated, and prepared to tackle life head-on. This time the angels weren't there.

Viola spent her early years in Bustamante, Mexico. Her mother died when she was only a girl, placing all family responsibilities solely on the shoulders of her father.

"Her father, unfortunately, couldn't handle his wife's death and became an alcoholic," Louis Barrios told me one afternoon as we talked at a quiet table in the back of one of his family's restaurants. "So she and her five sisters were left on their own."

Viola roamed here and there throughout her childhood, finally ending up in San Antonio, where she met José Barrios, a popular broadcast journalist.

"When my mother finally met my father, it was like, this was her stability, her rock," said Diana.

They had three kids and built a comfortable life centered on their family.

"We had the perfect parents. It would be almost sacrilege to complain about our upbringing—most people, they have one great parent. We had two," said Louis.

Fate stepped in when a drunk driver killed forty-six-year-old José on Labor Day, 1975. The family's dream suddenly became a nightmare for Viola, a new widow with three kids to support. After trying her hand at starting a few restaurants that failed, Viola scraped together $3,000 and opened the first Los Barrios restaurant in an old garage downtown. Other than the entrance, the restaurant was windowless. None of the furniture matched. But within two weeks, the place was packed. The enchiladas, tacos, and grilled fish were that good. And it didn't hurt that the restaurant was spotlessly clean. Soon, Viola moved Los Barrios into a space once inhabited by an old Dairy Queen on Blanco Road. That very location expanded into the family's flagship restaurant. All the while, Viola worked ten hours a day, seven days a week. The kids pitched in when they weren't busy with school and friends.

"My mother loved us selflessly, unconditionally, whether

we appreciated it or not. And sacrificially—she gave up her life for us," said Louis.

The kids grew up, had kids of their own, while Viola worked in the restaurant. Viola was the face of Los Barrios, cooking, checking on guests, ringing up bills at the cash register, always greeting customers with a warm smile.

Viola had an incredible way with food but there was much more to her success than the good cuisine people drove for miles to feast on. She welcomed customers as if they were guests in her home, making them feel a part of her family. She considered Los Barrios a family business that took care of other families as well. She often lent money and advice to her employees.

Her willingness to share didn't end at the restaurant. Each year, Viola and her daughter Diana taught a cooking class featuring their family recipes. Sometimes this was a little tricky since Viola kept most of her recipes in her head.

"Cooking for a loved one is a recipe for love," she'd always said.

Fortunately, Diana was usually able to come up with a written recipe that managed to capture the essence of what her mother instinctively knew. Proceeds from the class funded a scholarship in Viola's name, the Les Dames d'Escoffier Viola B. Barrios Scholarship. The scholarship, awarded to a female culinary student, encourages the practice of Mexican cooking and rekindles an interest in traditional foods and preparation techniques.

What's more, Viola always tried to be fair to her employees. Her kids recall the recent Christmas season when they discovered that a longtime employee had been stealing money from the restaurant. They wanted to fire the guy immediately, but Viola insisted that they wait until the holidays had passed, so not to ruin the man's Christmas. She was just that kind of person.

Several times a year, Viola would collect a Suburban full of clothes and other necessary items, take them back to Bustamante, the Mexican town where she'd spent her early years, and give them to people who were in need. Good deeds were her way of life.

Tragedy arrived in the form of an eighteen-year-old boy named Joe Estrada, who allegedly committed one of the most horrifying crimes I've ever come across. Estrada lived with his family in the house right next door to Viola's modest brick and stone home in northwest San Antonio. He had been an athlete at his high school, and hadn't given any indication that he was troubled. When his family moved into the neighborhood six years before, Viola welcomed them with homemade food.

Before the tragedy, Viola's kids had arranged for her to live in a huge house in a different neighborhood—a luxurious reward for all her hard work. She'd spent weeks packing her stuff. She was excited about the move, although she found it hard to part with anything, from drawings her grandkids had made to clothes that had clearly outserved their purpose. She was scheduled to move in two weeks.

Then, one night in April 2007, according to the criminal complaint, Estrada broke a window, climbed into Viola's house, and shot her in the head with a bow and arrow. Yes, a bow and arrow. The tip lodged deep within her brain.

The police believe the motive was burglary, but that things got out of hand after Viola woke up. After shooting the arrow into her temple, Estrada allegedly stole her car keys, drove to a gas station, bought a few gallons of fuel, then returned to the house and set it on fire. The police believe he wanted to destroy the evidence and make sure Viola was dead.

According to the charges, Estrada drove the Mercedes to the mall and bought some hair gel, an inexpensive laptop and camera, and some Guess clothes with one of Viola's credit cards. Within twenty-four hours, the police had charged him with murder. It was reported that Estrada confessed to burglarizing the house for money to buy drugs. Bexar County District Attorney Susan Reed, who had often eaten at Los Barrios and remembered Viola as a kind woman, immediately announced that she would seek the death penalty.

"I'd like to string this guy up myself," she said, with the San Antonio police chief at her side.

I've come across many murder cases in my years as a journalist, and usually the victim's friends and family don't have much problem with the idea that two wrongs *do* make a right. They usually want to kill or torture the murderer, trial be damned. But the Barrios children had a different reaction that struck me as pure, instinctive heroism that came straight out of their particular family dynamic.

Minutes after her mother's murder, Diana got a call saying her mom's house had caught fire. Fearing the worst, she sped over. On the way, she had the unworldly sensation of someone rubbing her shoulders, trying to make her feel better.

"I knew it was my mother, telling me everything was all right," she recalls.

At the house, no one seemed to know what had happened. The siblings stood together on the lawn. Later, they say, they all had the same feeling as Diana driving to her mother's house. The feeling intensified once they found out their beloved mother was dead.

"It's like we heard her loud and clear, and she told us, 'Forgive. Don't hate. I didn't live the way I did for us to feel this way,'" said Teresa.

And remarkably, that's just what the siblings did.

At a moment when many families would be beyond consolation and demanding revenge, the Barrios children established a nonprofit foundation called Viola's Huge Heart. The foundation has two objectives. One is to fund other nonprofits that are doing good work, such as the Les Dames d'Escoffier. The other is to turn Viola's family home in Bustamante, where her grandfather lived, into a health clinic or orphanage.

"We want to continue to help the people my mother helped her whole life," said Teresa.

On the third day after their mother died, the siblings did a TV telethon to raise money for Viola's Huge Heart Foundation. I know how difficult it can be to appear on live TV when your mind is clouded with details from your personal life, so it's hard for me to imagine how these three could have gone on TV so soon after their mother's death. But they did. And they raised a lot of money and awareness for the foundation. Many people said that watching the show changed their lives. Seeing the Barrios family gathered together with hope for the future made people reexamine their own bitterness, desires for revenge, and tendency to cling to anger.

It was remarkable how Viola's kids immediately offered forgiveness to the alleged killer and his family. They knew their mother was in heaven, and that the alleged killer and his family were going through what could only be hell on earth.

"You see this boy, and he's so small and he looks like he's only fifteen years old and you wonder, 'How could he have pulled this off?' " said Louis.

"I thought, 'Oh my God. If I had a child who did this to my neighbor who loved me and took care of me and helped me and welcomed me, how would I be able to live with that?' " said Diana.

"And you know what," added Teresa. "The amazing thing is that if our mother had survived she'd be visiting that boy in jail. She would be taking him fresh tortillas to eat. We're just fulfilling her way of living."

The only way the Barrios children could make sense of the murder was to imagine the heinous act as a tool God used to show the world the transformative power of forgiveness. If the children were able to use forgiveness and turn their mother's murder into a positive event, then the possibilities were endless.

"As strange as it may sound, we saw our mother's death as an opportunity for goodness," said Louis.

The opposite had occurred when a drunk driver killed Louis's father thirty years before. Louis had been a teenager then, and his heart filled with bitter rage at the man who was drunk and behind the wheel of a car.

"I was angry all the time," he said.

He spent years afterward following the dark path of drugs and alcohol. But when he was about thirty years old, Louis had a spiritual awakening and began to examine the concept of forgiveness. He spent the next three decades studying not just the Christian concept but reading about other religions and philosophies, too. In time, he realized that forgiveness is the key to removing the anger that had once led him into a self-destructive lifestyle.

"I came to see that forgiveness is a decision, not an emotion," said Louis.

Just as he forgave the man who killed his father, he forgave the boy who he believes killed his mother. And his sisters joined him.

They invited the alleged killer's parents to be the family's guests at Viola's internment. The young man's parents even rode in the limousine, with Louis, to the cemetery.

What's more, they met with the prosecutor and told her

they did not want Estrada to face the death penalty. They also offered to pay for his defense attorney.

"They told us it would cost a hundred thousand dollars to try this case," Louis said at the time. "The Estradas can't afford it. Well, the Barrios family can."

Of course, many people were baffled.

"Look, these parents felt so much shame. They had lost their son. Our mother was in heaven, but their son was clearly not," said Louis.

The city remained in a state of shock.

BARRIOS MURDER: SHOCKING TWIST, SPIRIT OF FORGIVENESS read the front-page headline of the *San Antonio Express.*

Not everyone viewed the world the way the Barrios siblings did. After the funeral, the family went to the restaurant Viola had first opened, where a Dairy Queen once was, so they could eat the food that their mother based their lives on, and collect their thoughts.

"One person, a family member, came up to me there and said, 'I need to talk to you about this compassion thing,' " said Diana.

Clearly, the fellow didn't approve.

"I said, 'My mother's death was negative enough. I don't need to add any more anger, any more negativity to her death,' " said Diana. "He just turned and walked away."

But that's how the family felt. Why make a bad situation worse? They didn't mind if other people reacted to their tragedy in different ways, but they didn't want to take that easy path, one steeped with anger and resentment. They knew their mother would never want that for them.

Their reaction to tragedy was one of the most heroic things I've ever seen. And the fact that it came naturally to the Barrios children makes it all the more remarkable. They never really discussed it. In fact, they don't seem to see what an amazing thing it is they've done. It's just how they were raised.

"There's nothing heroic about it," said Louis.

Spending time with the Barrios children is a real lesson in how to enjoy life, without being stuck in the past. It also shows how we can all live like heroes if we just choose to do what's right. The family was attacked in blogs, and by people they knew, for not being tougher, for not wanting vengeance, for not wanting an eye for an eye. But the children instinctively knew that in our time, where people seem to look for any reason to be offended, the spirit of forgiveness is powerful and sorely needed.

Their example has had a powerful effect. Since their mother was murdered, each one of the Barrios kids has gotten letters from people who were so moved by their story, that it helped them deal with forgiveness in their own lives.

"One person wrote and said, 'When you were at the church and you spoke on forgiveness, I felt something enter me and immediately I was able to forgive a person I had been holding something against for years,' " said Louis. "I've had people say that our example has changed their lives completely."

"Every day my patients talk about it, about something in their lives that need forgiveness," said Teresa, who is a podiatrist.

The Barrios children, through their actions, are spreading the concept of forgiveness. Like so many heroes, their situation was thrust upon them and it was something they never would have sought out on their own. How they dealt with the senseless murder of their mother is an inspiration that I can't stop thinking about. And I know it has something to do with the blood-bond that helps people stick by their family through thick and thin, through life, and, yes, even through death.

※

People often talk about how dysfunctional most families are. But it's all a matter of where you look. Sure, in my business I see people go through horrible situations. But I also see great stories of families that are more than functional.

Take the case of six-year-old Adrian Clark, who fell through a fourteen-inch concrete opening and into a fifty-foot-deep abandoned well while playing in Burnsville, North Carolina. It was early spring and the water was freezing cold. Adrian clung, shivering and scared, to the side of the well, about fifteen feet down the shaft at the waterline. He shouted for help. And it came to him in the form of his aunt, a fifteen-year-old girl with the unlikely name of Lykesia Lilly.

Many of these stories end badly. But this one doesn't. This

teenage girl's fearlessness in the face of a truly dangerous situation saved a life.

Quick-thinking Lykesia grabbed an electrical extension cord, peered through the well opening, and lowered the cord down to her terrified nephew. But he wouldn't grab it. He was too afraid that if he let go of the ledge, he would sink into the water and drown.

Lykesia tried to coax him out, but he wouldn't budge.

So she went in after him.

When I heard that, I wondered what I would do in a similar situation. We'd all like to think that we're capable of putting ourselves at risk for the sake of someone else, but, honestly, I don't think we know what we'd do until we actually face that kind of situation. I mean, lower yourself into a dark, cold well? I can't think of much that would be more terrifying to me.

Lykesia wasn't sure the electrical cord was strong enough to hold the child, but decided it was her best chance to save him. So she told the other people at the top of the well to hold on to it while she descended the narrow opening, using her feet and hands on either side of the walls to keep herself from falling. When she reached her nephew, she lowered herself into the frigid water. He managed a small, anxious smile as she whispered to him that everything would be okay. She tied the long cord around his waist and signaled the people at the top to pull him to safety. Lykesia waited in the dark well as she watched her nephew rise to the surface. Then she climbed out.

At the hospital, she was treated for cuts and bruises, but her nephew had no injuries whatsoever.

Absolutely amazing. Aunt Lykesia saw a crisis, and she responded to it with clarity and without hesitation. It was a good day for a family down in North Carolina.

Up in Berkley, Michigan, I met a man who told me a story that broke my heart and warmed it at the same time. Chet Szuber knows better than most anyone does just what it means to have your life saved by a family member. He's a Christmas tree farmer, so he's no stranger to heartwarming stories. But his will go down in history as one of the most unlikely tales I've ever heard.

When Chet was just thirty-six years old he suffered his first heart attack. At the time, his daughter Patty was just a one-year-old. He had two more heart attacks in the ensuing years, and Patty grew up with a father who was always expecting to die. As he got sicker, she helped him more and more, driving him back and forth to the Christmas tree farm and lending a hand wherever she could.

In 1990, Chet got onto a waiting list for a heart transplant but years passed and no heart became available. He could barely find the energy to walk and many times felt like giving up hope each time he struggled for a breath. Meanwhile, Patty, who had spent so much time taking her father to and from doctors' appointments, decided to become a surgical assistant;

it would be a good job that would give her the skills to care for her father. In 1994, a couple of weeks before she was to start school, she went on vacation to Tennessee. Their car didn't perform well on a tight curve in the Smoky Mountains and skidded off the road. Patty wasn't wearing her seatbelt.

Chet and his wife went to visit their daughter in the hospital, where doctors told them she wouldn't recover. In their devastated state, they found out she had filled out an organ donor card.

The doctors suggested they transplant his daughter's heart into Chet. Four days later, the spirit of his daughter Patty was beating inside his chest. He was the first person in history to transplant his own child's heart successfully into himself.

Now Chet is healthy enough to play golf. But it's hard for him to celebrate his new lease on life when it depended on his daughter's death. So he's dedicated himself to becoming an advocate for organ donors and transplants. To that end, he gives a dozen or so speeches each year to help raise awareness on how vitally important organ donation is.

Others can thank Patty, too. There's a woman in Nashville who got Patty's kidney. There's also a Memphis woman who received Patty's liver when the woman was only days away from dying.

Patty's a hero for caring for her father and taking the time to fill out that organ donor card, which helped her save so many people. And Chet is a hero, too, for honoring his daughter's sudden death with his dedication to raising awareness about organ donation.

"The time is always right to do what is right."

—Martin Luther King Jr.

Most of us can't imagine being in the same situation the Barrios children were, or what Lykesia and Chet went through in their own lives. But all of us, I hope, can look around at our families and know that some, if not all, of the people we love would go to bat for us in a pinch. And surrounding myself with this knowledge brings clarity to me in so many ways. What's more, it helps me set the bar for myself. I will step in and help whenever my family needs me. In our own little way, I believe that we all have the potential for such greatness.

Ordinary People,
Extraordinary Choices
You Make the Call!

You're standing at the back of the fish store examining the prepared foods when your cousin comes in dressed in waders, a vest dotted with hand-tied flies, and one of those goofy caps fishermen wear when they're wading in the rapids. He asks loudly if the store has any whole trout—"the bigger the better." He picks over what the store offers, choosing four fat ones.

"Take the heads off?" asks the fishmonger.

"Nope, those and the fins on, please," says the fisherman.

You're puzzled, thinking that with a getup like that he should have caught his own.

He turns to head out the door and sees you.

"Hey, how are you," you say.

He looks guilty.

"Doing great," he says, and walks on out.

You buy your pound of scallops and head out the door. Near your car you hear your cousin talking to his wife—loudly again—on his cell phone. "Yes, honey, I caught some big ones. I'm bringing 'em home right now."

You realize that he certainly saw the ones that got away, 'cause he didn't catch a thing.

YOU COULD:

A) Follow him home and tell his wife that she is married to a scoundrel.

B) Tell him to his face that you know what he's up to.

C) Get in your car, go home and enjoy your scallops, and the good story you've got to tell your friends.

D) Call the game warden and report him for fishing without a license.

This is an interesting situation with no clear-cut heroic moves. But for me, C is the best option. Sometimes a lie just doesn't mean much, especially if you're not involved in it. In this case, who would benefit from you telling your cousin's wife that he didn't catch a thing? It might just create disharmony in the family without accomplishing anything beneficial at all. As for telling him you know he's a liar, what's the point—he knows that well enough already. It might be fun to choose option D, but the warden probably wouldn't be amused.

CHAPTER SIX

Returning to the Scene of the Crime

I always try to get a window seat when I fly from New York to the West Coast because I love to look at the spectacular scenery below. The whole panorama of America unfolds, from the wetlands around JFK airport to the thick forests of Pennsylvania, the vast fields of the Midwest, the Rocky Mountain peaks, and the almost endless desert that leads into Los Angeles. I especially love the view when I stop a bit short of the Pacific and descend into the vast glittering cityscape of Las Vegas.

For most people, those lights mean fun. And I've had my share of parties, shows, and great meals in Sin City. But while reporting stories there over the years, I've learned that the lights tend to obscure a harsher reality. Only those who have lived in Vegas really know what I mean.

Vegas has always been a center of decadence. It got its name from the Spanish word for fertile field because the early Spanish visitors were drawn to its springs and oases, which provided respite from the harsh Mojave Desert. In the twentieth century, Vegas became a rough-and-tumble gamblers' mecca, where the drinks flowed all night and the buffets were endless. In the last decade, the city has lost some of its surface grit, as families discover it as a vacation destination, where kids can ride roller coasters, and folks can sit down to five-star meals in famous restaurants.

But, as is often the case, there's a world of pain beneath that exuberant facade. And a real need for good people to step forward and take a stand against the darkness that remains well hidden beneath the city's bright lights. Sometimes those who are best equipped to make heroic stands are those who have explored it themselves. They return to the scene of their own crime and make things better. There are more of them than you might imagine.

"You have not lived until you have done something for someone who can never repay you."

—Anonymous

I recently flew to Vegas to film a segment for *What Would You Do?* On my day off, I scheduled a meeting with one of Las Vegas's more interesting heroes, a middle-aged woman named

Jody Williams who lives with her teenage daughter far from the glittering lights, out at the edge of town where the cookie-cutter condo suburbs push right against the grit of the desert.

I left my hotel room and headed down the boulevard of luxury, known by all as the Las Vegas Strip. Driving past Treasure Island Hotel, where seventeenth-century sirens battle renegade pirates in a manmade cove several times a night, and the Bellagio Hotel, with its twenty-nine-foot-tall fountain flowing with molten white and dark chocolate, and past the fake Eiffel Tower at Caesar's Palace, I found it hard to believe that I was on my way to meet a woman who had dedicated her life to rescuing women—and some men—who had been trapped into lives of sexual servitude.

Las Vegas, with its exotic architecture, 24/7 casinos, and first-class restaurants, is also a center for prostitution. I've never understood the appeal of sex for hire. Early in my career, I spent years covering the wars in El Salvador and Nicaragua. The sex trade thrived there, with all the soldiers, journalists, and foreign workers living together in hotels. But I never took part in it. When I see a prostitute, I feel sorry for her. It's not a good life. And all fantasies aside, I don't believe there is any such thing as a "happy hooker." I wish more men would see things this way.

I can't imagine an America that would ever return to practice slavery, where humans were property. But the truth is, we're surrounded by a modern-day slave trade right now and most of us don't realize it. Gangs drag women and girls all over the world to work in brothels and clubs. When you see an ad in the back of a magazine advertising a "girl from the Orient," or a "barely legal cute blonde," chances are they've been coerced or even forced into the job. The traffickers kidnap, beat, rape, and psychologically torture women, and sometimes men, to get them into the sex industry.

Often, a young woman will be promised a good job, as a nanny or clerical worker, in another country, only to find when she arrives that she's expected to have sex with numerous men in order to repay the thousands of dollars she owes her smuggler. According to the U.S. State Department, eighteen thousand people each year are trafficked into this country, most of them women and children brought in for sex work.

Jody had given me her address but, thank goodness, I had a global positioning system in my car. Otherwise, I never would have found the condominium where she and her daughter rent a room, because they can't afford an entire place of their own. The condo was in a new subdivision at the edge of other almost identical subdivisions. All the houses looked the same. It was somewhat eerie.

It wasn't always like this for Jody, who led the high life back in the eighties. She was once known by the name Rene Chanel Le Blanc, and she ran a Los Angeles–area brothel that grossed thirty grand a month. This was back in an era before cell phones and personal computers were common, and since the brothel was equipped with closed-circuit TVs and Jody issued beepers to all the call girls, the newspapers referred to her as the "High Tech Madame" after she was busted.

"It was the most elaborate operation I've ever seen," said one of the arresting officers.

Jody reveled in her success. By no means does she try to make out that what she did back then was in any way saintly.

"But all the while I was in the business, women were coming to me for help in getting out of it—even when I was a madame," said Jody.

She'd help these women get out of the life because she has an intrinsic desire to help others. She attributes this core to her rough childhood.

"Sociopathic, child-molesting father, you know?" she said. "And my mom was a schizophrenic, with multiple personalities."

Somehow, Jody developed a feeling of empathy for others in similarly tough situations. She chose the perfect business for finding people in need. Men in need of sex and power. Women in need of father figures. Prostitution is a world of sadistic, often psychopathic pimps and criminals, where fear and disease are pervasive. People are sucked into this criminal universe, one singularly based on an elusive need for pleasure. People are trapped. Jody knows that most prostitutes would rather be doing almost anything else. But they get addicted to the action, and the power, and their ability to please others on demand. And their pimps convince them they aren't good enough to do anything else.

"Prostitution is not work," says Melissa Farley, a psychologist and expert on the sex trade. "Rather, it's a human rights violation."

Farley wrote a book, *Prostitution & Trafficking in Nevada: Making the Connections,* using statistics compiled by the State Department. She has no trouble equating prostitution with slavery. Right now, prostitution is legal in parts of Nevada. Proponents of legal sex-for-hire claim that it's cleaner and safer for the "girls" than the illegal sex trade since it's regulated by the state. But Farley says that's a myth, and she'd like all prostitution to be made illegal in Nevada. That doesn't win her any friends among the powerful who would like to see it legalized in all of Las Vegas.

I myself can't see how that would work. The U.S. Department of Justice has already put Las Vegas on its list of cities where human trafficking is a serious problem. There's no need to encourage more.

Still, even though prostitution has been proven to hurt most involved, it's not a very sympathetic issue. These victims aren't fuzzy little seal pups being clubbed by a ravenous mob. These are provocatively dressed women selling their bodies to people with emotional problems; it's not a good scene. Not many people are interested in helping prostitutes, much less people who are trafficked more like cattle than the human beings they are.

Jody's the first to agree. She knows it was wrong to have once worked as a madame.

After being busted and serving a few months in jail, Jody eventually left the business and became a paralegal. All the while, she occasionally got calls from women who needed help.

"At first I'd just get two or three calls per year from people who thought I could help them—it was really informal," she said.

Then, on August 15, 1987, the night before hippies and New Agers all over the world got together for what was billed as the "harmonic convergence," Jody had a powerful spiritual experience that was soon to change her life.

She'd been out of the sex trade for about two years. That night, she was in her bathtub when the whole room went blank and suddenly she was blinded by an overpowering white light.

"I couldn't even feel my body," she said. "Even when I shut my eyes, I saw white. Then I saw what I took to be an angel, all gold and white and about ten feet tall. I heard crying and sobbing in that light and I also saw blood flowing through the streets. A voice told me people were dying and I needed to do something about it. I needed to help those who still suffered."

Jody believed God had called on her to start a twelve-step program for sex workers, modeled after Alcoholics Anonymous. At first, she refused to listen. She thought, "Me? Start a twelve-step program? Are you kidding?"

Then God's voice told her that she had been freed from the

sex trade for a reason, and that was to help others in need. She shouldn't waste the opportunity given to her. Helping others was the price of her recovery. In an instant, the light and the voice disappeared.

It was soon thereafter that Jody founded Prostitutes Anonymous, since renamed Sex Workers Anonymous, a twelve-step program to help prostitutes free themselves from the business. Later, she founded Trafficking and Prostitution Services, or tapsdirectory.org, to assist sex workers who were held or trafficked against their will. She's always funded her own work, through her jobs as a paralegal and in advertising. But a few years ago, she became disabled from stress and other ailments and stopped work. Now she and her daughter barely get by on Social Security payments.

Jody thinks this drop of income was part of God's plan for her, because it is forcing her to expand her organization to receive funding so it can survive long after she's gone. Jody's training her daughter to run it, and she has big plans. She wants to build a community in the desert where people fleeing sex trafficking can live and learn new skills.

So far, she's helped thousands of people. She's bought plane tickets, rented apartments, paid huge phone bills, and stayed up countless nights helping others escape lives of degradation and exploitation, disease and self-hatred. She estimates spending well over $300,000 of her own money in her efforts. For that, she's a hero.

I spoke to one young woman who doesn't want me to use her name because she's struggling to put her years as a sex worker in the past, so I'll call her Laurie. "When I was a kid you'd never have thought I'd be a prostitute," she says.

She studied ballet. Got good grades. And scored very high on her SATs. Then, when she was nineteen, she had trouble finding a job. When someone said she could make good money as an exotic dancer, she started working the pole in a club. The money was easy. She was soon offered even better money if she'd do more than just take her clothes off onstage. And she realizes now that having sex for hire with men gave her more than just the cash she needed to get on with her life. It fulfilled her in unexpected ways.

"My father died of an aneurysm when I was twelve," she said. "I think I've always needed to replace him."

Natasha has a different story. She says she never got rich off her work, preferring to work just enough to get by.

"I didn't want to go out and get a regular job. I was very reclusive. Not highly sociable. If I could work an hour or two and make five hundred bucks, great," she said.

While Natasha says she didn't experience much violence while working, she got involved with a man who beat her regularly. That only fueled her sex work. The men who paid her gave her positive feedback, which gave her some semblance of the support she'd longed for at home, where she was being flattened, emotionally and physically.

"I used prostitution like a drug," she said.

About five years ago, she started feeling fed up with the life.

"I told myself I'd quit, but I couldn't," she says. "I got a license to sell real estate and to sell securities, but I wouldn't get a job. I'd just go back to the sex work. I kept saying to myself, 'What's wrong with me? Why can't I get out of this? I'm not stupid.' "

That went on until last year, when she came across Jody's website, sexworkersanonymous.com. She called the number, and Jody answered. Natasha told her about her life, explaining how she was in a relationship with a former client and that it was a disaster.

Here was this anonymous woman in the desert far away, but Natasha felt like she could talk to her about anything. She'd call Jody early in the morning, or late at night, and Jody always answered, always talked. There was never any question about her always being there.

"I felt really good after talking to Jody," said Natasha. "Somebody finally understood me. Sometimes we'd talk for hours."

Jody helped Natasha understand how sex work can be an addiction, and how she had a codependent personality.

"I'd always do thing for others, so I could feel better about myself," Natasha said. "Being with men was part of that. I realize now that it's addictive. That was an eye-opener to me. And Jody explained all these dynamics. She said it wasn't just about the money. She said there were lawyers doing it. Lobbyists in Washington, people who didn't really need the money. She said it was an addiction, for sure."

Jody and Natasha have never met. Their relationship is completely based on telephone and e-mail. Jody has dozens of relationships like this. She's gone into businesses and homes and rescued sex workers who are being held captive. And she's even hired gunmen to help her do it. But most of her work isn't that dramatic. Most of it involves listening, commiserating, and offering advice.

Natasha thinks she'd be in terrible shape now if it weren't for Jody.

"Jody gives me hope. She helps me understand the impulses that make me want to go back into the life," she says. "I'm just living hand to mouth right now, and it's hard. But she gives me ideas for jobs. For ways to change my life. And that's really important for anyone.

"I definitely think she is a hero. And right now she's the only one I've got," added Natasha.

Meanwhile, Jody continues her work. She knows she could have a better apartment, car, and lifestyle if she devoted herself to a more regular career and gave up trying to help people find new lives outside of the sex trade. But she can't.

"If I don't help them, who will?" she says.

Her name and number are passed around by word of mouth, along with people finding her on the Internet.

Her days and nights are very unpredictable. There was the night one girl called for help, but before Jody could rescue her, her pimp ran over her legs with a motorcycle, breaking both of them. Or the time a pimp poured gasoline on a girl and set her on fire before Jody could get to her.

"There are just so many stories," said Jody.

And that doesn't include all the threats she has received

from pimps, brothel owners, madames, and even the police and other officials and business interests who have a financial stake in prostitution.

"But it's a craziness I understand," she said. "The people in the business trust me, the sex workers, because they know I've been there myself.

"I've been very, very, very lucky," she added. "I mean I've literally had guns jam as someone was trying to shoot me. I know somebody upstairs is watching out for me."

Sometimes she thinks about giving up, starting a quiet life with her daughter.

"Then I get the next phone call. And I hear their voice, their need, and what else can I do but help?" she said. "We get those calls every day now."

"The best way to find yourself is to lose yourself in the service of others."

—Mahatma Gandhi

It takes a special person to return to the very place that negatively molded large portions of her past, as Jody has, to help others. To me, Cesar Chavez was one such hero.

When Cesar was fifteen years old, he took on work as a migrant farmworker, picking lettuce and beets. This is particularly backbreaking work, stooped labor for hours on end. Later, he returned to the fields to organize the same exploited workers into unions, so they could have some say in the quality of their working conditions, their pay, and ultimately their dignity.

I know something about migrant labor. My father was out of work in the spring of 1967, and we needed money badly. When the neighbors told us about a caravan of migrant workers headed north to harvest fruit, my parents pulled me out of school in May and we piled into the '55 Chevy and headed north, too. I was thirteen and this was my very first trip out of Texas. I was excited. We drove pretty much nonstop in a long line of migrant-filled cars and trucks, led by a supervisor who covered all our food and gas.

But somewhere outside of Indianapolis, we were separated from the caravan, and suddenly we were lost in what seemed like a foreign world. We stopped at a Catholic church and my mother, feeling embarrassed about what had happened, went in to talk to the priest. To this day, I have no idea how she communicated since she spoke such limited English. But he gave her money for gas, a loaf of bread, and a gallon can of green beans. That lasted us two days, and kept something in our stomachs until we regrouped with the others in the caravan.

Finally, we made it to Northport, Michigan, where we picked cherries for six weeks or so. It was beautiful up there, with crisp air that I'd never experienced before. But the work was brutal, every day picking cherries for pennies. Each evening my mom would make us some tortillas and beans, and we'd crash on cots in a tiny room set up for us.

When the cherry-picking season was over, we moved south with the caravan to Swanson, Ohio, where we harvested tomatoes for Hunt's Ketchup. For the first fifteen minutes or so it felt like a brush with fame—Hunt's Ketchup! We ate that at home! I became a legendary picker, within my own family, because I could load 120 bushels a day. At thirty cents a bushel that came to thirty-six bucks for a twelve-hour day, which was quite a lot back then.

The brutal work saved our family that summer. And it taught me that I didn't want my future to be one of following the next crop. I decided that summer to do whatever it took to go to college.

Cesar Chavez knew that not everyone had the same determination that filled me after working such a summer, or the good luck. In 1962, along with Dolores Huerta, he founded the National Farm Workers Association (later renamed the United Farm Workers) and started one of the greatest civil rights movements in American history. At a time when cities in America were burning from riots protesting racism and the Vietnam War, Chavez led nonviolent protests.

The NFWA supported Filipino harvesters when they went on a "grape strike" in California in 1965, demanding better wages and working conditions. He led a farmworkers' march to the state capitol in Sacramento. He urged Americans to stop eating grapes in support of these workers. The boycott was amazingly successful, with everyone from Kansas schoolkids to Senator Robert Kennedy offering support.

Conditions for the laborers improved.

Chavez devoted his life to this kind of work, and improved the lives of hundreds of thousands of farmworkers in the process. While he had the skills to go out and do anything, he didn't flee his family's migrant roots. Rather, he returned to that difficult place that formed who he was. As far apart as Jody and Cesar's lives may seem, they have followed parallel paths in my mind. Both have gone back to help those who remind them of their own struggle. That's courage.

I was fortunate enough to meet Cesar toward the end of his life. And I felt humbled to be in the presence of this true American hero, one who kept close to his roots. He's been one of my inspirations ever since.

"Who indeed can harm you if you are committed deeply to doing what is right?"

—I Peter

Over the last decade, I've done several interviews with a vivacious young woman named Melissa Wall, whose experience I'll never forget. If I hadn't known her story, there's no way I would have thought this heroic woman, who seems to have so much love for life and hope for the future, had been the victim of one of the most destructive religious frauds the country has witnessed.

Melissa grew up in an outlawed and renegade polygamist sect of the Mormon Church. When she was just a girl, the sect's "prophet," a man named Warren Jeffs, told her father he wasn't good enough to raise his kids, and he put them in the care of an older polygamist.

Jeffs ran a small empire out of his walled compound in a remote part of the Arizona desert called Colorado City. Everything in town was under his control, from the local police to the owner of the convenience store. Jeffs decided who lived where and who would marry whom. Anyone who defied him, he said, would be defying God.

When Melissa was fourteen, Jeffs ordered her to marry her first cousin, whom she despised.

Until her wedding night at the isolated Desert Hot Springs Motel, in Caliente, Arizona, Melissa had no idea what sex was.

"I didn't know anything about anatomy—even my own," she said.

Warren Jeffs had banned sex education of any kind from her school.

But that night her cousin began her initiation. They moved into her stepfather's house, along with twenty wives and dozens of children. Over a period of years, her husband repeatedly raped her.

"This was part of my religion," she told me. "This is what I was supposed to do. I was supposed to be happy fulfilling the word of God."

But she was miserable. Finally, she couldn't take it any

longer and one night she fled into the desert in her truck. At the very moment when she began to suffer her fourth miscarriage, her truck broke down. She lay on the desert floor in the middle of nowhere expecting to die. Another child of polygamists found her. This young man, Lamont Barlow, had been banished from the sect as well. Together they fled and established a new life together.

But Melissa didn't just hide. She stepped forward like a true hero. After Warren Jeffs was arrested on two counts of rape, Melissa testified against him.

"I looked him right in the eye and didn't flinch," she said.

She still doesn't flinch. Or run. In 2008, when four hundred children were removed from the polygamist Zion ranch in Texas, children born to polygamist women, some of them just teenagers, Melissa volunteered to counsel them. She traveled to Texas and helped these young women through their crisis. And she'll continue returning to the root of her darker history, that chapter in her life involving polygamous exploitation of young girls, if anyone needs her. Melissa has empathy, courage, and plenty of experience to know that sometimes you just need a helping hand. In other words, she's a hero.

"The world is a dangerous place, not because
of those who do evil, but because of those
who look and do nothing."

—Albert Einstein

Sometimes a hero just seems to spring out of his environment, adapting to the climate as needed. Like Julio Solis. He thinks of himself as a bad-ass who drag races through the desert near his hometown of Puerto San Carlos, the small fishing town on the Pacific coast of Baja California, below San Diego.

He smokes. He drinks. He's an unlikely hero.

This part of Baja is a naturalist's paradise. Offshore, one finds whale calves, along with a myriad of other incredible fish. Onshore, it's the wild west. Until recently, people didn't pay attention to fishing regulations, much less the environment. The entire area was a hotbed for drug use and smuggling.

Like others in his community, Julio was never much concerned with the environment. Now he's on the board of Vigilante de Bahía Magdalena, a watchdog group set up to protect the Bay of Magdalena. He is the executive director.

Julio was hanging out and trying to earn a living when he started driving a motorboat at the School for Coastal Studies, a research outfit that used the bay for study. Working with the scientists, learning about the area's endangered sea turtles, and discovering how vital the bay was to his community transformed him into an activist. He realized he had to think about the future and not just that night's party.

"I'm still a rebel, but now I'm a rebel for conservation," he brags.

Magdalena Bay, with its mud flats, sea grass, beaches, and

mangrove forests, is one of the most important wetlands we have. Many people make their living fishing its waters. And, besides the sea turtles, many threatened birds make their home in and around the bay, including brown pelicans, frigates, and bald eagles. The Pacific gray whale raises its young there before traveling north to the Bering Sea. Lately, its beauty has drawn developers. These new resorts and condominiums add to the runoff and untreated sewage that is polluting the bay. Sometimes the shore near the fish cannery is slick with green algae, all feeding on the waste in the water.

Julio has dedicated his life to preserving Magdalena Bay. He gets death threats because he opposes huge new developments. Many of his peers criticize him. Some of his old compatriots who poach fish don't understand his way of life. But he's glad to be on the same water he's always enjoyed, only this time he knows he's on the right side of the line.

"All serious daring starts from within."

—Eudora Welty

In the 1980s, I spent years covering the wars in Central America. The brutality I saw, particularly in El Salvador, was stunning as the U.S.-backed government fought Marxist guerillas. Many local families immigrated to the United States.

And some even sent their children alone to places like Los Angeles, believing it would be safer for them there than in their war-torn homeland.

Susan Cruz was part of this wave of war-scarred immigrants. She arrived in Los Angeles with her mother when she was eight years old. She found a city that didn't want her. Even other Latin Americans seemed to look down on the recently arrived El Salvadorans.

"It was a hostile environment," she said.

Early in her life in the United States, Susan was playing at school when the kids around her took up a game of four squares. She'd never heard of the game and didn't know the rules, let alone enough English to play it. The kids teased her. And then a girl with blond hair and blue eyes walked up and punched her in the face. Susan had never been hit like that before. She fought back. And because she couldn't explain to the principal, in English, what had really happened, she was suspended. Her mother was furious.

She quickly learned to hang out with her own kind—other kids from El Salvador. They could commiserate about their lives and the difficulties of living with parents still recovering from the posttraumatic stress disorder brought on by the violence of El Salvador's civil war.

Susan's mom was strict. Susan made it through junior high and high school without getting into trouble. But she got close with a group of neighborhood kids, who had joined a gang called Mara Salvatrucha 13, or MS-13. In El Salvador, "mara" is slang for "a group of friends," and "Salvatrucha" is slang for "El Salvadoran." And the number 13 is a prison signifier for people from Southern California.

"My mom, like many Salvadorans, hates the gangs with a passion," said Susan. "She ranks them right up there with the El Salvadoran death squads during the war. That bad."

According to the FBI, MS-13 is one of the most violent gangs in the country, with members who are quick to take up arms. Almost all the early members were immigrants from El Salvador. Now, as members have been deported from the States or gone back to other Central American countries, the gang has spread. There are an estimated ten thousand MS-13 members in the U.S., according to the FBI's Mara Salvatrucha task force. Tens of thousands more are spread throughout Central America and even Europe. Many MS-13 members have covered their faces with elaborate, intimidating tattoos that can scare the most hardened criminals.

The gang has many offshoots and there's no centralized command, although many individual chapters are highly structured. According to the FBI, the gangs generally get money by extorting funds from Central American businesses, everyone from construction companies to the small fruit vendors on the corner. They've also branched into human smuggling, bringing illegal immigrants into the States for high fees.

Some crimes attributed to MS-13 include the murder of a seventeen-year-old girl for snitching to police, taking over a

Honduran bus and killing twenty-eight passengers on board, most of who were women and children, with machine guns, and killing a man and his two sons after they got into a minor traffic accident with a gang member in San Francisco. The violent list goes on.

When she was nineteen, Susan rebelled against her mother's strict limitations. She left home. And she started hanging out with her friends in SM-13. It was only a matter of time before she was a member.

Little did she imagine that the price of being in the gang was attending funerals at least once a month, witnessing one of her homeys commit suicide and die in her arms, and getting shot herself ten days before she was arrested. That arrest happened one afternoon when she drove six guys from the gang to a beach near L.A. to resolve a beef that had arisen with another gang that had stabbed an MS-13 member. One of the members in her gang shot his gun into the air. They piled in the car and she sped off. She, as the driver, and the shooter were charged.

The shooter saw his potential prison sentence as a great thing for him, like a scholarship to the Harvard of the streets. Susan was devastated. The arrest was the first her mom knew about her being in a gang. It horrified her. Susan was upset when she saw her mother's distraught face in the courtroom. She was given two years.

When she got out of prison, Susan moved in with her mother. But her mom was difficult. She didn't trust her and wouldn't even give her a key to their home. Applying for jobs was a nightmare, because as soon as Susan told people she'd done time, they lost interest. Soon, she rejoined the gang. But even that life was difficult. In time, she realized that if she remained a gangster, she'd end up in prison again and probably fall into a rotating cycle: gangster, prisoner, gangster, prisoner, dead.

In 1992, the El Salvadoran government signed a peace accord with the rebels and the war ended. Susan had longed to see her homeland for years, so she returned and got a job with an American trading company. By that time, MS-13 had spread throughout Central America, and many former Los Angeles gang members had been deported back to the country. While she didn't participate in any criminal activity, she did hang out with them.

After three years of living in El Salvador, she grew tired of the sexism she felt was inherent in the culture. She wasn't sure about her job, either, which mainly involved importing equipment for the military and police—many of whom she found to be scarier than the MS-13 bangers she'd known. She was a native El Salvadoran, yet she had been raised largely in America. She didn't fit in anywhere. She decided to return to Los Angeles.

Back in the States, Susan worked for a couple of anti-gang organizations. And then in 2000 she founded Sin Fronteras, which means, "Without Frontiers."

"I wanted to give some of these kids that lift I hadn't always had," she said. "I wanted to help them avoid the life I had found myself in the middle of."

The all-volunteer nonprofit organization was meant to focus on the most vulnerable kids: children of immigrants, undocumented minors, kids in foster care. Susan and the other volunteers offer workshops and classes that help with the basics: how to apply for a job, how to make a budget, how to apply to community college, issues with relationships, understanding grief and mental health, sexual health, and other topics. There are now about a dozen active volunteers, working with about three hundred at-risk kids each year. All the volunteers have other jobs. No one is paid for the work they do with Sin Fronteras—not even Susan, who supports herself with other work.

But their work makes a difference and helps former gang members find their way in a world that doesn't look too kindly on them.

Sin Fronteras goes into jails and helps kids be rehabilitated. The organization helps undocumented immigrants with their legal problems. And it tries to be there, as an understanding presence, whenever immigrant gang members, or kids who are heading that way, need help.

Susan wants to help these kids climb over the barriers that stand in their way as immigrants. She offers them career counseling, conflict resolution training, and other skills, with the hope of reducing violence, homelessness, incarceration, and increasing the self-esteem and independence of those she works with.

Sometimes the most difficult circumstances to overcome are deeply embedded into the roots of our past. For many, even being born in the wrong place, at the wrong time, without a strong support system and no clear options is too much to overcome.

Susan Cruz knows this and can see beyond it. She's heroic for passing that hope along to countless kids who might otherwise get lost in the system. She returned to the scene of her crime—in her case being a gangster—and turned it into a positive experience for so many.

The same can be said for Jody and Cesar Chavez, and the many others we all come across that have turned their harsh experiences into the positive drive needed to change the world around them.

Ordinary People, Extraordinary Choices
You Make the Call!

On your way to the train station to catch the 7:17 into the city, you stop at a vending machine to buy the paper. Digging in your pockets you feel lucky to come up with the exact change: 75 cents. The headlines look bad as you take the paper out, but what happens next seems even worse. Just as you start to close the vending machine a well-dressed man stops the door from closing and says, "You don't mind, do you?" as he reaches in and takes a paper for free.

YOU COULD:

A) Let the door slam sharply on his fingers and walk away laughing.

B) Pretend you don't hear him and walk away.

C) Call 911.

D) Calmly tell the man that you don't think he is doing the right thing.

Obviously, A is the correct choice—not. While the thought of maiming a miscreant is enticing, it might land you in the slammer, or the very least have you facing a lawsuit. B is the easy—and the wrong—choice. Calling 911 might seem productive, except that you might be wasting the operator's time when she could be dealing with a more urgent matter, like a murder or a fire. For me, D is the best choice. You can't force the man to behave, but you'd be right to let him know that what he's doing violates your—and the community's—moral code.

CHAPTER SEVEN

Keeping Order in the Chaos

S o often, admirable people rise from the depths of the most miserable situations. That was the case in Ciudad Juarez, Mexico, when in 1996 I went to investigate a series of puzzling murders that occurred there. I had heard reports that scores of young women had been killed, often in horrific ways, over the years in and around this booming border town of one and a half million people. Since my first visit, perhaps three hundred more women have fallen victim to a killer or, more likely, killers.

To put that in perspective: Ted Bundy confessed to killing thirty women. The Boston Strangler killed thirteen. And Jack the Ripper lives on in infamy for just five murders. There's no agreement on who is responsible for the Juarez atrocities, though everything from a *chupacabra* (mythical "goat sucker"), to drug smugglers, to serial killers from the United States has been blamed.

JOHN QUIÑONES

The victims were almost all young Mexican factory workers in maquiladoras, plants that U.S., Mexican, and international companies have set up along the border to take advantage
of low wages and access to markets guaranteed by the North
American Free Trade Agreement. The killers often cut off
the women's hair and mutilate their bodies. It was possibly
the most prolific killing spree of its kind in world history.
And no one—not the Mexican police, the maquiladora owners, or the local government—seemed to be doing anything
about it.

But a hero rose up out of this nightmare of violent neglect.
Vicky Caraveo took it upon herself to organize a group called
Mujeres por Juarez to search for the women's bodies and raise
awareness of the terrifying crimes being committed against
women in Juarez. She wanted to give the dead their proper
respect. And she wanted those who were still living to be re-
spected, too.

Juarez is a vast, chaotic product of globalization, and the
cross-cultural exchange that has made the border of Mexico
and the U.S. almost a world unto itself, with different mores,
ways of speaking, and communities. There are more than
three hundred factories, or maquiladoras, located in the Juarez
area, and they operate 24/7, cranking out products for the rest
of the world. Big corporations build them in Juarez because
the labor is cheap and the regulations are lax. They can get
away with more than they could across the border in El Paso,
Texas.

Many bodies are required to keep this machine churning and several hundred thousand people a day enter the factories. Many of these workers are young Mexican women struggling to help keep their families afloat. They come from the interior of Mexico, from impoverished farms and ranches where they can no longer make a living. They board buses and journey hundreds of miles to find jobs just hundreds of yards below the U.S. border.

The new factory recruits offer an endless supply of young victims for the murderers.

I met one young woman named Hortensia. She arrived in Juarez with dreams of a good job and a better life.

"Back in my hometown, it's impossible to find work," she said.

At the time, she was paid about $3.50 a day, which wasn't enough to rent a decent apartment. So she ended up living in one of the colonias, or shantytowns, that ring the city. Hortensia shared a shack with no running water or electricity with her mother and father and two sisters. It's a typical story.

Juarez is a big city, with several wealthy neighborhoods where the streets are smooth and the gardens are well tended. It also has sprawling neighborhoods of cheaply built cement brick houses, where water is delivered by truck because there are no pipes and where electric lines are rare. And these are the middle-class areas. Then there are the colonias, like Anapra, Lomas de Poleo, and Felipe Angeles. Felipe Angeles is absurdly located directly across the Rio Grande from the

University of Texas at El Paso, with its picturesque campus. Destitute families can look out their front doors, over the deadly no-man's-land, and gaze across the river upon the verdant lawns of American higher education.

I know the Rio Grande well. It's not very wide. In fact, I crossed it in a little boat with some illegal immigrants one time, while working on a story. When I reached the other side, I checked into the El Paso Hilton, while the others disappeared into the undocumented darkness. That narrow, shallow river might as well be an ocean, for the vast difference between the life of the Mexicans in Juarez and the life of the Americans in El Paso.

Everyone needs a champion. Some people could use one right away.

In the poor neighborhoods where the maquiladora factory workers live, homes are often just pieced together from whatever is at hand. The walls are made from wooden shipping pallets from the factories, or abandoned bedsprings, or thick pieces of cardboard wrapped in plastic. If they are lucky, a family will find a sheet of metal for their roof. Inside, the floors are often dirt. The kitchen is a propane burner like the one you'd use for camping. There's a plastic container for water. Some bags to hold whatever food is available. Children play in the dusty yard—often thick with toxic white powder or effluvia from the factories—alongside emaciated dogs.

But strangely enough, these barrios are still places of hope. In most cases, people came here because the factories offered more than what they could get in their villages. So amid the misery, there is fulfillment. Unfortunately, that satiety only lasts for a while. And after a few months, or years, being poor in Juarez is as insufferable as it is anywhere else.

In this environment, there's no way that a young woman would refuse to work in the maquiladoras, just because a few hundred girls have been murdered. They need the money too much.

On the same trip, I met a girl named Guillermina. Her sister, Sagrario, had been murdered a few months before while walking home from work.

"We're poor, so we have to keep our jobs no matter what happens. That's the curse that we face," Guillermina told me.

The maquiladora workers take one of three shifts that fill the twenty-four-hour clock that rules every factory. They make cruise-control systems for cars, or sandals, or shiny toys. And those who work the second shift, from 4 p.m. to midnight, step from the factory into the forbidding desert darkness, headed back on buses and desolate footpaths to their shantytowns. One night I followed Guillermina from her job to her home. It had been less than a year since her sister died taking the same route.

At 12:25 a.m., Guillermina boarded a bus near her maquiladora for the half-hour ride to downtown Juarez. My crew followed her with a hidden camera as she walked through the red-light district, with its bordellos and prostitutes, drunks and drug addicts, gangsters and shadowy men. She had no choice but to pass through there to get the bus to her barrio.

"It's a great risk to walk these streets," she said. "The lack of security, it makes me so nervous. You must not show your fear, even though you're very afraid."

At one thirty in the morning, she boarded another bus for the forty-minute ride to her shantytown. It was after two when she got off the bus. That's when the most dangerous part of her journey started. The walk through the desert, all alone, in the darkness. At least eight bodies of young women had been found along the path that Guillermina walked each night.

"With every step you take, you say, 'Thank God, I'm alive. I wonder if I'll still be alive after the next step.' You leave your house, and you don't know if you'll ever return," she said.

Generally, the people living in these broken-down barrios are nearly invisible creatures. The power elite of Juarez doesn't notice them, unless they don't show up for their shift at the factories, or as maids in fancy homes, or to dress up in clownish costumes and stand on street corners selling lottery tickets to wealthy people passing by in their cars.

That's why it was so surprising to people when Vicky Caraveo got involved with the slums. She's one of the people in the fancy cars. Her grandfather was a Mexican general, and she's part of the Juarez upper crust. She lives in a big house in a country club neighborhood. If she wanted to, she could bask in the sun all day and eat bonbons all night. But she has a heart as big as Mexico. And she empathizes with the plight of the people. As described in the book, *The Killing Fields: Harvest of Women*, by Diana Washington Valdez, Vicky first became an activist to protest high electric rates that she thought

were milking the poor. She led demonstrations. And in soli-
darity, she lowered the lights in her own house until the rooms
were practically dark.

In time, Vicky also became interested in how propane was
marketed to poor people, who were completely dependent on
it for cooking. She felt the propane companies were charging
too much for the gas, and she organized protests. What a shock
it must have been for the wealthy people she went to school
with to see her rubbing shoulders with the working class and
striving to help the poor get fuel to cook their beans and toast
their state-subsidized tortillas. This was not where a Mexican
woman raised in a life of privilege was supposed to be.

When Vicky was appointed to head the Chihuahua State
Women's Institute, she met some of the women from Anapra,
Felipe Angeles, and Lomas de Poleo. When she heard their
stories about losing their daughters, she was horrified. Realizing that the powerful and wealthy of Juarez, including some
people in her own family, don't care about poor women, she
founded Mujeres por Juarez, or Women for Juarez. She took it
upon herself to empower the powerless. That's true heroism.

The murders had started in 1993; by 1996, it seemed that at
least fifty women had been murdered. Many of them had been
tortured and mutilated. Since the police seemed to be doing
little to investigate or stop the murders, Vicky and other
women started searching the poor neighborhoods and outly-
ing desert areas, looking for victims and gathering evidence.

During one of these sweeps of the desert, the group discov-

ered a small shack made of concrete blocks. It appeared abandoned. But just outside they found a mound of what looked
like human hair. And inside, they found women's underwear
and other clothes. And there were bloodstains on the floor.
The scene was shocking. And strangely enough, there was a
piece of wood leaning against the wall.

None of the searchers had ever come across anything quite
like this piece of wood. The board was covered with detailed
pencil drawings, as if done by a madman, or by a woman being
held captive. There were odd drawings of nude women. Their
hands and feet were indistinct, but their eyes, breasts, pubic
area, and hair were all shaded in. There were other drawings
of soldiers in tight formation. The mountains outside of
Juarez. A cactus. An ace of spades. Marijuana leaves. A Star of
David. And Nazi swastikas. Vicky was appalled.

When she called the deputy attorney general for the area,
he tried to blow her off. She and the others gave the board,
with the drawings intact, to state investigators. After a time,
the state officials came back with their verdict: the blood on
the board was pigeon blood. They had nothing much to say
about the drawings or the hair Vicky and the searchers had
found. It seemed they didn't want to deal with the reality of
femicide.

As Vicky knew, the powerful and wealthy of Juarez weren't
interested in these poor women. There were always more
where they came from. Why worry about losing a few?

When I first met Vicky, I was struck by her resolve and her
passion for a cause that was so far outside her social realm.

Her heroism came from compassion, empathy, and courage. No one knew if it was one serial murderer, a gang, or just an ever-expanding psychosis among the population that was leading to so many deaths. The crimes seemed unfathomable. As the number of killings grew, women began to report that their husbands would cite the crimes during arguments to scare them. As in, "You better behave or I'll dump you in the desert."

A typical murder went like this: A thirteen-year-old girl we'll call Rosales arrived in Juarez from her home outside of Durango, Mexico. She moved in with her brother, who worked in a factory, and used the fake ID her parents had given her to get a job of her own. She'd been in Juarez for less than a month when her body was discovered in a lot on the southwest side of the city. She was raped and suffocated with a plastic grocery bag. It turned out that she'd gotten off work the same morning she was found dead. So her killer must have abducted her in broad daylight.

"It's horrible the way they torture our girls, and then kill them. It's not normal," Vicky told me, her green eyes projecting a mix of shock and anger. "Sometimes they're completely destroyed. The only things left behind are the bones and certain garments."

I spoke to the head of a group that represents the maquiladoras, many of which are American-owned. The man, Robert Urrea, struck me as indifferent to the problems. He's president of a trade group that represents the factories. I asked him why he didn't change the girls' work hours, so they didn't have to walk home at one or two in the morning after taking buses to the colonias after their shifts.

"If you restrict the hours you're working, you're going to restrict the economic influx into that city. And there's a reason—there's a reason that these companies are in Mexico. And you've got to understand, this, John, is to be globally competitive," he told me.

In other words, it wouldn't be cost-effective to cancel the late shifts, even if it might save lives. Urrea even suggested the victims might have asked for trouble and brought the murders on themselves.

"Where were these young ladies when they were seen last? Were they drinking? Were they partying? Were they on a dark street? Or were they in front of their plant when they went home?" he asked.

This got a rise out of Vicky.

"Sometimes they try to justify this, saying that the girls go to the bars at night, go dancing, when the only thing you're doing is going to work. It makes us very mad," she said.

"When we think of the sky, we tend to look up, but the sky actually begins at the earth."

—Diane Ackerman

Amnesty International doesn't blame the murdered women. This organization says the violence against women in Juarez, and in Chihuahua City, a few hundred miles away, where similar murders have occurred, is very complex. According to Amnesty, there are most likely a number of murderers with different motives. But they are able to operate because the cities tolerate violence against poor women, and because the police and courts won't punish anyone who is responsible. In a study, Amnesty found that the families and activist groups, such as Vicky's, have worked incredibly hard to bring the murders to the attention of the world and that this, more than anything else, is working in favor of the threatened women. But not everyone likes the attention.

By the time of the march, Vicki's group had done twenty-seven sweeps of the desert, looking for bodies. They'd generated tons of publicity and had tried to work with the factories, the police, and the judicial system to end the killing. In 2003, a group of people marched 250 miles from Chihuahua to Juarez in protest. When they reached Juarez, local thugs attacked the group, knocking Vicky to the ground.

One day I went with Vicky to the desert to look for bodies. At the time, they would find a new body about every two weeks.

"The persons who are killing our girls came here, killed them, tortured them, raped them, threw them away, and nothing happened," Vicky said, as we walked through the dusty colonia. "The murderers have to know the place perfectly. They have to know because they come during the night."

Vicky and the others seemed indomitable as the search progressed.

"We are the people of Juarez and we got together and came here to look for more victims. That's the only reason anyone has found them. We're the ones."

"Not the police?" I asked her.

"Not the police. They never have found a body. Only the people have found the bodies."

Walking through here in the footsteps of the women who've disappeared can be a frightening experience. It is eerie and desolate, almost as if there are ghosts all around us. Imagine how it feels if you're out here alone, and you know a serial killer is on the loose.

As we walked, one member of the group, a woman named Lupe, tried to read some footprints she found in the sand.

"Do you think there are more bodies out there?" I asked her.

"Yes," she said. "But out here, as you can see, if a woman screams, who can hear her?"

Well, I thought, Vicky Caraveo hears these women. And she bravely does her best to help them and prevent further murders in the future. It's a tough job. The Mexican government eventually let the FBI come in to advise local authorities. And some progress has been made. But as recently as 2007 over twenty-five more women were murdered in and around the colonias of Juarez.

During one of my visits, thousands of citizens of Juarez joined activists in a nighttime vigil and protest. It was quite a sight. Over 25,000 candles were lit that night, and the flickering flames cast a hopeful light over the throngs.

"It is beautiful. So beautiful," said Vicky. "This is not politics. This is not a movie, you see. This is real life."

The real life of yet another hero that I'm so lucky to have spent time with.

The mayhem in Ciudad Juarez is in a class by itself. And I'm grateful that Vicky and many others like her have taken it upon themselves to step in, when the people who are paid to protect the young women of the city have failed them miserably. Vicky's job is ongoing and requires great diligence and foresight. But sometimes a crisis comes upon us suddenly and there's no time to plan a response.

"Bravery is the capacity to perform properly
even when scared half to death."

—General Omar Bradley

I heard a wonderful story about just such an occurrence during one of my trips out West. I was reading the Las Vegas newspaper when I came across the story of a homeless man who saved a little girl from certain death.

If you've ever been to a desert city like Las Vegas, you'll understand just how difficult it is being homeless in such an environment. The summer days are brutally hot, with temperatures hitting upwards of 110 degrees F at times. The sun glares down relentlessly and the endless boulevards have very few shade trees. When winter comes, a cold wind blows off the desert that can numb you to your bones. Las Vegas isn't very pedestrian-friendly, either. Getting from here to there can require navigating under highway cloverleaves and crossing busy intersections.

Homeless people in Las Vegas tend to congregate in parking lots during the day, especially near Dumpsters that might provide food, or where passing motorists might slow down and hand out a dollar or some change. At night, they sleep on sparsely trafficked sidewalks. It's not unusual to see a vacant block that's packed with makeshift tents and sleeping bags come nightfall, as the homeless, who don't have much use for or access to the clubs and casinos on the glittering strips, can settle down for a relatively peaceful night, protected by each other. But mostly, homeless people in Vegas are like they are everywhere else: invisible. The average Joe on his way to work at a mall barely notices them.

That doesn't apply to the mayor of Las Vegas, an entertaining guy by the name of Oscar B. Goodman. He spent thirty-five years defending "reputed mobsters," as he put it, before becoming mayor. Under his watch, the city banned handouts to homeless people in parks. And even though there's a severe shortage of space in shelters for Las Vegas's estimated fifteen thousand homeless people, he suggested making it illegal for them to sleep outdoors. He even went so far as to say that panhandlers holding up signs saying they're hungry should be sued for "false advertising" because they can get free food at soup kitchens.

But the mayor might want to pause and consider the heroism of one of his constituents, a forty-eight-year-old man named Stan Washburn. A while back, Stan lived across from the Silver Nugget Bowling Center, in a vacant lot littered with cigarette butts, bags, and old wine bottles. Sometimes he'd come across a dead rat. At night, Stan would crawl into a little hole he'd dug into the dirt. Down there, the wind wouldn't hit him.

One Saturday afternoon, not too long ago, Stan was sitting on a wall near a Jack in the Box restaurant drinking some beer with other homeless buddies. Empty cans of Steel Reserve 211, a potent malt liquor, littered the ground around them.

At about 2:30 p.m. he noticed a young girl standing at the edge of a crosswalk with an older woman. To his shock, the girl suddenly bolted into the street and right in front of a Cadillac. The driver hit his brakes, but the girl had already been dragged under the car.

"No," she screamed. "No."

The older woman screamed along with her.

Stan stood up, ran over to the car, and tried to lift it. When it wouldn't budge, he called his friends over to help.

"Let's go," he shouted.

They all rushed over together, leaving half-empty cans strewn on the ground.

Under Stan's guidance, they picked up the rear of the car and moved it to the side. Once the weight was off her, the little girl started to breathe. Soon, paramedics arrived and took her to the hospital.

Stan later told a reporter for the *Las Vegas Review-Journal* that he could see his own young girls in the eyes of the girl trapped under the car and that gave him strength.

"I mean, I knew it wasn't one of my girls, but I remember them when they were that little, and I knew it was somebody's little girl. I was devastated by the accident. I just couldn't let her die," he said.

Stan didn't stop to think that day in Las Vegas. He just felt the need to help another. In a city that doesn't appreciate his kind, Stan Washburn is a true hero.

※

Not too long ago I visited Las Vegas. As I drove toward the Silver Nugget Bowling Center, I imagined what this man must look like: tall, dressed in ragged clothes but somehow keeping his dignity. I wanted to take him out to dinner, or for a cup of coffee. I wanted to give him a few bucks to help him on his way to wherever he was headed. But the vacant lot was empty. A windblown monument to another one of America's unsung, but to the people who know him, definitely appreciated, heroes.

Ordinary People, Extraordinary Choices
You Make the Call!

Sitting at your dinner table with a roast and a good bottle of wine, you and your husband are startled when the chandelier goes dark. It takes a second to realize the whole apartment is dark—no TV, computer, lights or stove. The romantic candles you lit save the day, and it seems like it will be a beautiful evening. That is, until an hour or so passes and you start hearing craziness on the streets outside your building. It looks like some people are getting ready to do more than just enjoy the stillness of the blackout—you fear a riot might be developing. You're scared, remembering the looting that has happened in previous blackouts.

YOU COULD:

A) Barricade your front door and hide out in your apartment until everything passes.

B) Call the police.

C) Gather stuff together to throw off your balcony at people if they get out of hand in the street below.

D) Gather up all the candles you have and go down to the street and try to calm the situation by passing them out to people in need.

One thing I've noticed is that some of the most surprising acts of heroism are based on spontaneous acts of kindness that seem to have a ripple effect. You do one good and surprising turn, and many more seem to follow. That's why answer A is probably the least useful and definitely least heroic of the choices. It is focused inward, on your own safety, rather than outward, towards your community. B is a good idea, but chances are that in a situation like this the police will already be overwhelmed with calls. C would be fun, for a while, but somebody could really get hurt, and I doubt you'd accomplish a thing. Answer D might seem a little crazy, but for me, it's simple and beautiful—you put out good feelings and you're likely to get them back.

CHAPTER EIGHT

Risking Your Life for Another

Twenty-year-old Jeremy Hernandez wasn't feeling at all spectacular on the sunny day when fate called him to risk his life for the sake of another—actually, make that fifty others, all of them children. Instead, he was sleeping in the back of the bus.

It was August 1, 2007, a typical day of a typical Midwestern summer in Minneapolis. Jeremy was the gym coordinator for a group of kids ranging in age from kindergarten to high school at Waite House Neighborhood Day Camp. His job was to play games with the kids and help with the swimming classes. He loved it even though most days he came home completely exhausted.

Jeremy spent that morning giving swimming lessons to fifty-two kids, which would be enough to wear out even the hardiest person. The bus driver, a woman named Kim Dahl, was taking them back to the camp's home base at Waite House when traffic slowed to a crawl. The eight-lane bridge they were taking across the Mississippi River was being repaired, with several lanes closed, so the rush-hour traffic had to squeeze into a tight space.

The work had been going all summer, as huge crews of more than a dozen guys with jackhammers pounded away at the concrete. So the traffic wasn't a surprise. But the bridge collapsing was. It fell right out from under them and into the Mississippi River.

Thirteen people died in the tragedy, and nearly a hundred, including twenty-two children, were treated at hospitals. There could easily have been fifty more casualties, all of them kids. But there weren't, thanks in great part to Jeremy.

What a way to wake up.

Bridge 9340, as it was officially known, was built between 1964 and 1967 to carry highway I-35W across the Mississippi River in Minneapolis, and just below St. Anthony's Falls' lock and dam. The 1,907-foot bridge had fourteen spans, including three long main spans that rose over the rough waters downstream from the falls. The structure wasn't what you'd call a work of art, like the Brooklyn Bridge or the Golden Gate Bridge, but it was well used. Before Bridge 9340 collapsed, about 140,000 cars crossed it on a typical day. If you lived in the Twin Cities, you'd have used it. There's no other option.

Minneapolis and its sister city, St. Paul, suffer incredibly cold and icy winters. Whenever I'm there between November and March, I long for the healing warmth and sunshine of

Miami or points farther south. But most Minneapolitans seem to love their winters, and they do a lot to adapt to them. Up there, people even plug in their cars during the coldest months to keep the oil in the crankcase from getting too sluggish. The locals are tough, and they're used to hazardous conditions. Even so, Bridge 9340 was known as a danger zone.

One year it was named the most treacherous cold-weather stretch of freeway in the Twin Cities. That's because some combination of how it was constructed, the wet wind of St. Anthony's Falls, and other factors made it common for a layer of thin black ice to form on the roadway when the temperature dropped below 30 degrees, which is often. Cars routinely spun out on the black ice and collided with one another.

To counter this, in 2000 the Minnesota Department of Transportation installed temperature-activated nozzles to spray the surface with a de-icer when it dropped below freezing. Some people think this chemical might have weakened the bridge. Apparently, there were cracks and corrosion visible on the underside of the bridge. And perhaps the weight of the cars and the workers, and the jackhammering, had weakened the bridge more than anyone imagined.

"The important thing is this: To be able at any moment to sacrifice what we are for what we could become."

—Charles DuBois

Whatever the cause, at 6:05 p.m., the long central span shook and there was a huge rumbling. But it wasn't like the famous video of Galloping Gertie, the bridge that in 1940 started swaying in gale force winds over the Tacoma, Washington, narrows, until it undulated like a ribbon in the wind before collapsing. No, the Minneapolis bridge just fell in one flat piece, like a cracker falling from your hand to the floor. The entire middle section went into the river in one awful moment, sending shock waves of water high into the air. One driver said he felt the road bend and twist, and then suddenly all the cars ahead just vanished. Behind him, the broken roadway went downhill until it connected with the riverbank. He backed down it to the end. Looking through his windshield, he saw the cars farther up sliding toward him. They crashed into a pile nearby.

A video of the collapse shows the whole thing happening in a matter of seconds. Suddenly, there were cars in the water, trucks dangling off the edge, cars stranded on chunks of concrete. There were people swimming. People fleeing. Others were running to help. On land, terrified people screamed. In the water, victims tried to claw their way out of cars. Frantic men and women shouted into cell phones everywhere, overwhelming the 911 switchboards.

There were many heroes that day—the civilians making 911 calls, the divers braving treacherous currents, the police, the firefighters—but Jeremy stands out.

It was Wednesday, the kids at Waite House had gone to a

big water park, and everyone was worn-out from the sun and fun. Headed toward home base, Kim, the driver, downshifted into the bumper-to-bumper traffic. They were running late. Her own two kids were with her on the trip that day, but she worried that the other parents might start to worry.

As they inched along a section of the bridge that spanned the riverbank with a good view of the waterfall upstream, one of the kids woke Jeremy. So much for his nap. He looked out the window at the waterfalls below. Then the concrete turned to Jell-O. The span bent, and the bus careened downhill as if it was on skis.

"I thought I was dreaming," Jeremy said.

The section they were on split from the roadway and dropped about twenty feet, sending the bus careening to the side.

Jeremy Hernandez was wide awake now.

"It was almost like a wave happened and the whole bridge went down," Kim said. "I mean we were just going straight down, not knowing what was happening, just scared to death."

The bus fell with the roadway.

I can't even imagine.

The bus and its section of roadway fell until one end crashed into the riverbank and the other end dangled from broken bridge parts above.

"It felt like we were on a roller-coaster ride at Valley Fair and my stomach was in my chest and I was waiting for it to stop," said Jeremy.

Kim slammed on the brakes, not knowing what else she could do. The bus slammed against the guardrail, a truck, who knows. There was broken glass everywhere. The bus came to a stop at the railing, finally. The railing held firm. They were not going to tumble off the bridge.

Kim realized she couldn't feel anything in her legs. She was injured. But the kids were her first priority. What a relief, then, to have Jeremy Hernandez on board—even though he still didn't know he was about to become a hero.

Dust filled the air. A semi nearby burst into flames. The kids started screaming. One teenager used her cell phone to call her mom. She got voicemail.

"Mom, answer the phone, it's me," she cried into the phone. "Momma. Momma."

Jeremy was scared, but he didn't have time to think. As the dust settled, the view got clearer and he could see the disaster: rebar sticking up from chunks of concrete, twisted steel, smashed cars, people wandering the bridge.

"We're going to go in the river, we're going to go into the river," some kids screamed.

When some others heard that, they started screaming, too.

"We're going in the river!"

"I looked over at the water and my heart started beating fast," Jeremy said. The bus felt like it was still moving. He didn't want to die on this bus. And he didn't want to fall into that river. He'd swum in the Mississippi before, and he knew it was powerful. It was at that point that he made a courageous decision.

In some ways, it wasn't even a decision. It was just instinct.

"I jumped over the seats, and I opened the emergency door
and kicked the coolers that were blocking it out of the way."

He could have jumped out and run for his life, saved himself and to hell with the others. But he didn't.

The possibility didn't cross his mind. Not with all the kids
on the bus.

"They're like my brothers, my little sisters. I've been working here for years, I feel like they're a part of me. Every day, I
come, I come to see 'em, their smiles," he said.

Not to mention the other counselors. And poor Kim, the
bus driver, who was hurt.

The kids surged toward the open door. A man came to the
back of the bus and Jeremy started handing kids off to him.
Throwing them really. He was that desperate to save them.
The kids lined up together along the edge of the bus. Jeremy
could still feel the bridge shaking. Who knew if it would collapse further?

"You got to get off the bridge, you got to get off the bridge,"
he shouted at the kids.

More people ran up and Jeremy kept handing kids to them.
Ten, twenty, thirty, the kids just kept on coming.

"I just remember grabbing one and then putting them
down, grabbing and then putting them down," said Jeremy.
"It felt like it went on forever."

The children were screaming and clutching any adult they
could reach. They were sure they were going to die.

"It was terrifying," said one of Jeremy's fellow counselors. "But our bus was one of the lucky ones. People died in that collapse. It felt like it was a miracle we didn't."

Jeremy says he was just glad to be able to help. And lucky to be alive to see another day.

After he got all the kids safely off the bus, along with the counselors and the driver, Jeremy took a careful look around to be sure none of the kids had strayed from the group. He looked at the semi that burned uncontrollably nearby. He looked at the block of cement that had fallen on another vehicle. He looked down toward the river where rescue workers were struggling against the current to find survivors. He felt blessed.

Jeremy stayed at the disaster site until every single child was either reunited with their parents or taken to the hospital. When he got home, he realized how much his own hip and leg hurt. But other than that, he was fine.

A hero? He didn't think about it, but I have. And I'm here to say that he is. I'm proud to breathe the same air as this guy.

"Our prime purpose in this life is to help others."

—Dalai Lama

Here's another person I admire: Philip Bevacqua, a fellow who was trained to be brave. But he didn't have to risk his life once he retired as a captain in the police force in Paterson, New Jersey. After twenty-five years, he'd seen his share of insanity and had been in many dangerous situations. Then he left the force and forged a life with regular hours and fewer lunatics. But one July evening, the seventy-seven-year-old Philip was sitting on his back deck having tea and cake with friends when he heard gunshots. It was as if he was still on the force. He immediately went to the front of his house to see what was happening.

It was a fellow officer in the street out front. John Sole was fighting with Peter Riva for a gun, his uniformed sleeve soaked in blood from where he'd been shot twice.

"Put it down, put it down, put it down," Officer Sole ordered the man.

He didn't respond.

Philip wasn't the only witness. Several other people who heard the shots were gathered nearby. But no one did anything to help the officer. Not only did this violate Philip's code as a police officer—albeit retired for many years—but it also went against his conscience as a human being. So he ran up, grabbed the guy, and punched him.

The man hit back. But Philip got in more good blows. At last, the assailant staggered away, gun in hand, probably wondering what kind of planet this tough old man came from.

That's when Officer Sole was able to pull out his own gun and shoot the guy.

Philip's clothes got soaked in blood. There was so much of it that some of the bystanders thought he had been shot, too.

Officer Sole and Riva went to the hospital. Philip just went back to his house and got cleaned up. He realized he hadn't really thought much about what would have happened if he'd been shot. Once a hero, always a hero.

※

But there's a first time for everyone. We all wonder if those smoke alarms in our homes will wake us up if there's a fire. Well, in 2005, Billie Meade's woke him up at his home in Jackson, Michigan. The problem was it took him a few groggy moments to realize what that weird sound was. He got up and found that the hallway outside his apartment was filled with smoke. So he woke up his girlfriend. They got dressed. Billie grabbed his favorite possession, a black leather motorcycle jacket, and they went out to the balcony of their second-floor apartment. Billie jumped. Then he called to his girlfriend to jump—he was going to catch her. And he did. But that wasn't enough. The building was still on fire. An image of his ninety-year-old neighbor came to his mind. What if she didn't know about the flames? What if she was trapped? What if there were others like her? Risking his life, Billie went back into the burning building to tell the others to flee. He pounded on doors and yelled for everyone to get up and get out. He ran into a neighbor in the hallway who was disoriented by the smoke so he guided him out. He still hadn't seen his ninety-year-old neighbor so he pounded on her door. When she didn't answer, he broke the door down. As smoke filled her ground-floor apartment, he got her to safety through some sliding glass doors.

Billie was honored by the local chapter of the Red Cross for his efforts. He lost almost everything he owned that day. But he found so much courage in the process. He could have lost his life. Instead, he saved several others.

"Like the body that is made up of different limbs and organs, all moral creatures must depend on each other to exist."

—Hindu proverb

One amazing hero did eventually lose his life defending against the depredation of the Amazon rain forest. Chico Mendes was born into a family of rubber tappers in the state of Acre, Brazil, near the borders of Peru and Bolivia.

Tapping latex for rubber is an intensive process. First, you carefully cut a line into the bark of a rubber tree, being careful not to cut through the cambium, the thin layer between the bark and the wood that makes the tree grow. In the bark, there are microscopic channels that carry the latex. When you cut these, the white, creamy latex drips down the gouge you've made and into a cup.

Early every morning you must visit each tree to remove any latex that has clogged the cut. When you come back about four hours later, there should be enough in the cup to harvest. On a plantation, a worker could harvest hundreds of trees in a day. If the trees are wild, then he'd have to wander through the forest and the number would be far fewer. Clearly, it's intense work. That was Chico's life, starting from age nine.

But when he was in his twenties, rubber prices plummeted. Many landowners sold out to cattle ranchers who cleared the trees so the cattle could graze. Suddenly, men whose families had worked the rubber trees for generations, often in conditions resembling slavery, were out of work and kicked off the land where they thought they'd always live. It was wrenching.

In time, Chico and some of the other tappers started protesting by invading the areas where ranchers were clearing land, convincing workers not to continue and even disarming the guards. As you can imagine, they angered a lot of people in the process.

Then Chico really started causing trouble, at least in the eyes of the landowners and cattle ranchers. He entered local politics and started advocating for something called "extractive reserves." Families who made their livelihood by harvesting latex, nuts, and other forest things would manage these protected forests. He started the Xapuri Rural Workers Union to unite local people against the ranchers. Soon, he formed a large union, to bring together all the tappers across the Amazon. Tappers traveled from all over the country to attend the first meeting, in Brasilia, a city in the middle of the forest that had been founded by robber barons in the previous century.

It was the 1980s, and cattle ranchers, settlers, and others were burning the forest at a rapid clip to clear land for agriculture. On the ground, the forest seems endless. You can walk a hundred yards into the Amazon forest and feel like there must be trees for miles around you. It's that thick, and back then the forest did go on almost forever. But I remember that if you flew over the Amazon at night, you'd see an inferno of almost unimaginable proportions. Parts of the forest below would be a seething cauldron of red-hot flames. There wasn't an unlimited supply of forest. And Chico knew this. The tappers needed those trees. The world needed those trees.

"At first I thought I was fighting to save rubber trees, and then I thought I was fighting to save the Amazon rain forest. Now I realize I am fighting for humanity," he said.

In 1988, the situation in the Amazon finally entered world consciousness. The public in America and Europe, as well as in the sophisticated neighborhoods of Brazilian cities like Rio de Janeiro and São Paolo, began to believe the scientists that had been warning of environmental disaster if the forest was destroyed. They predicted global warming, depletion of the soil, starvation, and other catastrophes. They said the forest might disappear before all the medicinal plants there could be catalogued, let alone utilized.

All this empowered Mendes. He wasn't a charismatic guy, but he was determined. Already, ranchers eager to raise cattle had kicked around 100,000 tappers out of the forest. Chico fought back with protests and publicity. He even had families stand in front of bulldozers to stop them from ripping trees out of the ground.

He flew to Washington, D.C., to meet with officials at the Inter-American Development Bank who were financing a new road into Acre that most environmentalists feared would lead to an influx of settlers who would further deplete the forest. The project was cancelled, angering the powerful ranchers, politicians, and others who would have earned a lot of money from it. He won several awards and got a ton of publicity in the international media for his efforts. Chico was well on his way to becoming a folk hero.

After returning to Brazil, Chico pushed the government harder to create the forest reserves he had long advocated. The ranchers fought back. One particular rancher named Darcy Alves Pereira decided to go ahead and cut trees on land that Chico hoped would become a reserve. Chico fought back, and halted the clear-cut. This act might have been his undoing. On December 22, 1988, Chico opened his front door and was killed by a shotgun blast. He was forty-four years old. Two years later, Pereira, the rancher, and his son got nineteen-year sentences for their role in his murder. Many people think others were involved. And the death threats continued against Chico's widow and some of his coworkers. An activist priest was shot. Chico risked his life to save the forest and the liveli-hoods of the people he'd grown up with. Sadly, it was by losing his life that he made the most impact.

Chico's murder was on the front page of every major news-paper in the world and the injustice of it galvanized the envi-ronmental movement. The Brazilian government cut off tax subsidies to Amazon cattle ranchers. The military even sent helicopters to put out rain forest fires. A reserve was created in Chico's name in Acre. Dozens more followed. Who knows if that would have happened if this hero had not given his life?

※

Curtis Dawson, of Astoria, Oregon, wasn't planning for the ensuing danger one winter night when confronted with a po-tential disaster on the Columbia River. This river is vital to commerce in the northeast, and it stretches from British Co-lumbia, in Canada, down to form the border of Washington and Oregon states before emptying into the Pacific. It carries the fourth largest amount of water of any river in the United States, and it is one of the most powerful streams of water anywhere. You have to be strong to work a boat on this river.

Forty-seven-year-old Curtis was an assistant engineer on a tugboat that was moving a barge along the river on December 3, 2005. A sixty-seven-year-old man named David M. Schmel-zer captained the tug. It was nighttime and they were working during the ebb, or outflowing, tide, when the currents are especially swift. Curtis was on the barge, with the tug close by.

Suddenly the tug capsized in the rough current, turned upside down, and broke free of the barge.

Curtis saw Schmelzer floating, unconscious in the water. Without a second thought, Dawson jumped fully clothed into the frigid water and swam to where his captain lay, near death, his face in the water. He pulled up his head and held on to his jacket. Meanwhile, the barge and the tugboat were drifting off and the current was carrying Curtis and the captain away. Using powerful strokes, Curtis swam toward the barge, pulling Schmelzer with him. A deckhand on board saw the rescue and tossed them a line.

Another deckhand grabbed the first hand's legs as he leaned over the side of the barge to pull Curtis and Schmelzer from the water five feet below. They eventually got the captain on deck. Curtis climbed up after that, numb with cold. A helicopter whisked Schmelzer to the hospital and then came back for Curtis. In the end, both men were fine. For his unblinking willingness to risk his life in the service of another, Curtis was awarded a Carnegie Medal for Extraordinary Civilian Heroism. A high honor, indeed. But nothing compared to the satisfaction of successfully rescuing his captain.

Would you risk your life to help another? We'd all like to know if we have it in us, and while I hope most of us do have that capacity, I also hope that brand of heroism isn't tested too frequently.

Ordinary People, Extraordinary Choices
You Make the Call!

It's Friday night and your country house beckons. You pack the kids and the dog and your spouse into the car and get onto the freeway for the three-hour drive north to the lake. Everything seems great except the traffic, which is unusually intense. About an hour into your drive you see a car zigzagging ahead of you. It appears the driver is drunk. Suddenly the car veers into the next lane and forces another car to go off the road and hit the guardrail, skidding to a stop with a thud. Smoke is pouring out of the hood. You know something bad has happened. People could be hurt. No one else is stopping.

YOU COULD:

A) Drive on by. You've got a car full of people and you know someone else will deal with it.

B) Note the mile marker and ask your spouse to call 911 and tell them where the problem is.

C) Pull over and see if there's anything you can do to help the injured passengers.

D) Put the pedal to the medal and chase the drunk driver.

Sadly, these kinds of accidents are all too common. In this situation, A is definitely the wrong choice. Even those of us who are not heroic by nature need to learn to act when another person's life is in peril. Choice

B would be sufficient, and might make the most sense because you have your kids in the car with you—do you want to risk their lives too by pulling over in heavy traffic next to a burning car? I think C is the heroic option, but it's not for everybody—and if it's not for you, then B is definitely the answer. D would be heroic in a Hollywood action movie, but for anyone in real life it would be the foolish response.

CHAPTER NINE

Good Business

I've reported stories amid some of the worst poverty on earth: in a neighborhood suspended on stilts above raw sewage in Port au Prince, in sprawling refugee camps in the Central African Republic, and even here in America, in forgotten, destitute towns in the Mississippi Delta and on Native American reservations in the Southwest. I've seen three-year-old children snapping rags and buffing shoes to get a little money for their families—a desire I'm familiar with, though I didn't try shining shoes myself until I was ten years old. I've seen mothers forced to choose which one of their kids would get a bite to eat that night, because they didn't have enough to feed them all.

Sometimes I've been right there with these people, reporting from the slums and sleeping in them, too. But just as often, I've lived a life of privilege in the midst of the misery, staying at whatever local hotel caters to foreign journalists, eating in restaurants where wealthy executives dine. The chasm between wealth and poverty startled me at first. After a while, however, it began to seem almost normal.

After spending years in places like Nicaragua, it seemed like an intractable human condition. When you see so much poverty, you began to think that's the way the world is: a matter of business. Often I've wondered why, with all our technology and all our expert businesspeople who so deftly pile up money right and left, there are still so many people living in such dire straits. Too often, business is a self-centered game. Money is the goal, the social contract be damned. I don't want to become that jaded.

Which is why it was so refreshing to learn about Muhammad Yunus. He figured out a way to help millions of people around the world rise out of poverty. And it all started with just $27 from his own pocket—less than many Americans spend on Starbucks in a week; I'm sure there are some who spend that much in a day.

Muhammad's goal is to eliminate poverty from the face of the earth. It's as simple as that. This is no pie-in-the-sky dreamer, here, either. He really thinks we can do it. And given his success so far, I'm starting to believe him.

Muhammad was born the third of fourteen children in a small village in a region of British-controlled India called East Bengal. His father was a goldsmith, who pushed him to get an education and gave him lessons in money. His mother ran the home and had a habit of assisting every poor person who ever knocked on her door. Their example would lead him to change the world. Or at least the lives of millions.

In 1969, Muhammad won a Fulbright scholarship to study economics at Vanderbilt University, in Tennessee. By that time, India and Pakistan had gained independence, with the latter country absorbing East Bengal. The per capita income was about $360 a year. Sixty percent of the people lived well below the poverty line. Since Bangladesh is one of the most densely populated places on earth, many poor people were shoved up against one another. The farmland of Bangladesh is fertile but only because it's mostly delta land, which means it's subject to frequent monsoons, cyclones, and vicious floods. We've all seen the video clips of people walking down country lanes, the water up to their necks, a pot of grain balanced delicately on their heads. It happens almost every year in Bangladesh. Still, it was Muhammad's homeland. He felt lucky for his life of relative privilege, studying at Vanderbilt and getting to know the United States. He wanted to give back to his people by returning home to teach college economics after getting his PhD in America.

In 1971, the people of Bangladesh, angered by what they saw as discrimination and economic neglect from Pakistan, started a war for independence and the country of Bangladesh was established. Muhammad returned, hoping to help his country evolve into a better place. At first, euphoria ruled.

"But things went downhill fast," he said.

Almost immediately, the new state faced starvation, devastating floods, and military coups d'etat. In 1974, the country suffered a devastating famine and Muhammad came face-to-face with the horrors of poverty in ways he'd never seen before. Bangladesh's infrastructure had been ruined by the war. It was the poorest country in the world, and he felt like their society was just starting all over from scratch.

To him, all the grand economic theories he'd learned at Vanderbilt seemed pointless in the face of the misery around him. He had a crisis of confidence.

"Then I got the idea that if I can change even just one little thing to help just one person just a little bit for just a single day, that would be enough," he said.

As an academic, Muhammad wanted to find comprehensive solutions to multilayered problems. Now all that changed. He began to notice how poor people suffered tremendously from problems that could be solved with just a small amount of money.

When it was necessary, they'd borrow what they needed at high rates from thuggish moneylenders, who'd then own them, in effect, and any work they did. One day Muhammad met a woman who had a small business making bamboo stools. She told him she only made a profit of two to three cents per day for her work. He was shocked. She explained that since she'd never been able to put together the twenty-five cents she needed to buy the materials to make one stool, she had to borrow it from the lender at rates as high as 10 percent a week. In return, he made her sell the stools to him at a price that he set. There was no way she would ever be able to get ahead, and it was all because she lacked a tiny amount of money. For twenty-five cents, she'd be able to get out of debt. And she'd be able to charge a decent price for her work.

When Muhammad asked around the village, he found that there were forty-two other people in similar straits. Their total combined need was just $27. For that relative pittance, they were stuck in poverty, and so were their families, probably for generations to come.

"I took twenty-seven bucks from my pocket and told them to pay back the lenders and then sell their stuff in the market for higher prices, so they could buy more materials to keep working," he said.

It was an act of pure selflessness.

But it was not charity. Heroism is often a product of realism. Muhammad is a clear thinker. Handouts or welfare, which he feels damages a person's dignity and keeps motivation at bay, does not impress him. So he provided his $27 as an interest-free loan that the villagers could pay back at their convenience. They were incredibly excited.

"It gave me a sense of liberation," he said during one interview. "Like it was a miracle. An offer from heaven. I thought, 'If you can make so many people happy with such a small amount of money, why don't you do more of it?' "

He went to a bank with the idea of convincing them to make small loans, similar to the one he'd just made. They told him that was impossible because poor people are not creditworthy.

"How do you know that?" Muhammad asked.

"Because I do," the banker said. "They'll just spend it and never pay it back."

"They pay back the moneylenders," he said.

"That's because they'll get beaten if they don't," said the banker.

Frustrated, Muhammad offered to guarantee the loans, and he cosigned all the loan papers. There were people wanting to be food vendors, basket makers, rice pounders, and all manner of other trades. And they were able to get started with these small loans. He was amazed at how these tiny amounts of money could change their lives. One woman bought a cow, and after selling the milk for a year, she owned the cow outright. From then on, all the milk, and any calves, were pure profit. It was that simple to create entrepreneurs who were motivated by the possibility of pulling themselves up from destitution.

In 1983, Muhammad convinced the government of Bangladesh to let him form the Grameen Bank. "Grameen" means village, and the bank was set up to be owned 10 percent by the government and 90 percent by the borrowers and depositors. In other words, the poor would own their own bank, which had four founding principles: discipline, unity, courage, and hard work.

If those principles don't define heroism, I don't know what does.

Over time, Muhammad found that loans made to women had a greater benefit for the families than loans made to men.

So the bank began to specialize in lending to women, and now over 90 percent of their borrowers are female.

Often, at the bank's encouragement, the women will organize themselves into groups of five or so. Then the group can borrow the money, each member will prod the others, and together they'll figure out how to make more money and repay the loan. In the process, they often do some community work, such as advocating for good hygiene, family planning, and other services. It's almost like a heroism virus that spreads outward from group to group, from community to community. Muhammad's impulses are contagious.

The bank has grown tremendously in the last twenty-five years and now it has over a thousand branches serving millions of borrowers in tens of thousands of villages in Bangladesh and elsewhere. Amazingly, 98 percent of the loans are repaid, which is far higher than the rate at conventional banks. Since opening in 1983, the bank has lent a total of about $6 billion and that figure is rising rapidly. It's at the point now that the bank lends about $800 million each year, in loans that average about $100 each. The bank makes a profit and finances itself, which is amazing. It exemplifies Muhammad's idea of making "not for loss" organizations rather than "not for profit."

"Lend the poor money in amounts which suit them; teach them a few sound financial principles and they manage on their own," Mohammad has said.

And now that system is being applied in dozens of other

countries, including the U.S., Canada, France, Bolivia, and elsewhere. Muhammad says that more than a hundred million people worldwide benefited from Grameen's system of micro lending.

"Poverty is a denial of human rights," he said.

And he aims to use good business to wipe these human rights violations off the face of the earth. Muhammad has said that he plans to eliminate poverty, in all forms, in all countries. And he plans to get halfway to his goal by the year 2015. That's not too far away.

Right now, about half of the people in the world live on less than two dollars a day, and perhaps a billion of us live on less than a dollar a day. I'd say it's heroic to be able to hold up your head and be optimistic under those conditions. In America, we forget that most people on earth are poor. And most of them are women and children. We don't stop to consider them as we go about consuming all the things we think we need.

We might benefit from paying attention to this humble man's audacious goal.

"I want a world where no one lives in the misery of poverty, and where our children will have to go to a museum to know what poverty is. They will look at the displays and be angry at the previous generations for allowing such a thing to exist," he said.

Muhammad is a rare combination of pragmatism and lofty goals. He remains upbeat, despite the work ahead of him. He believes that humans are wonderful creations, full of possibility, and capable of miracles. But, he says, so many of us are never allowed to unwrap our gifts. So many of us die without knowing how much potential is inside of us. He believes that micro lending allows people to begin to understand their capabilities, and be empowered by the feeling.

In 1986, Muhammad and Grameen Bank were awarded the Nobel Peace Prize. Immediately, Bangladesh erupted into a spontaneous celebration lasting for three days, with people filling the streets and most commerce in the country shutting down due to the people's joy. Some said it was the most celebrated event since the country's declaration of independence.

In his book, *Banker to the Poor*, Muhammad asks whether it is possible to imagine a world without poverty. And then he answers: "We have created a slavery-free world, a polio-free world, an apartheid-free world. Creating a poverty-free world would be greater than all these accomplishments."

Muhammad believes that, in today's world, access to credit is a human right, like the right to work, eat, have a home, and get health care. But he knows that only with credit are the other rights attainable.

A poor person is like the seed of a giant tree growing in a flowerpot, he says. You can have the best seed, but unless you give it a large base, it will stay small. He believes the same is true for people. You have to give them the opportunity to grow. And if we, as a culture, do that, we'll be taking a big step toward becoming, for the first time, civilized human beings.

It started with the simple idea to help one person a little bit for one day. And now his contribution is spanning the globe. That makes Muhammad a true hero to me.

☀

I have a sneaking suspicion that we are going to see creative capitalists like Mohammad in the coming years. All around the world, business leaders are beginning to realize that there's more to work than just making a buck. Even Bill Gates is in on it. In fact, he's one of the leaders of the movement called creative capitalism.

I'm sure some of the most innovative capitalists will come out of the Wharton School, the business program of the University of Pennsylvania, in Philadelphia. Over the years, this school has graduated thousands of incredibly successful businesspeople like Ron Perelman, John Sculley, Donny Deutsch, and many others. While Wharton graduates have already proved themselves adept at minting the green, I think many future graduates will show themselves to be unusually adept at integrating their work lives and personal lives in ways that help make them, their families, and society at large happier and more productive. I respect that heroism.

No doubt, Stewart D. Friedman will be a key player in that effort.

Stewart is a professor at the Wharton School and is a bit outside the mold of what you'd expect a business professor to be. He's a good-looking guy, animated and cheerful. Nothing stentorian about him. And he makes his students do the strangest thing: they must talk about the intimate details of their lives, their goals, and how they'll achieve them. So it's not just about making the Benjamins. It's about quality of life, too. For some people, the whole idea is scarier than an IRS agent with a vendetta.

By the way, the course is required.

It has such a transformational effect on the students that Stewart has developed a following—groupies—who treat him like a rock star. The kids are tired of a business world where work takes precedence over everything else, including your family, and the pleasure of living well. They want to integrate their personal and career lives into a more organic whole. Stewart encourages them. Even forces them to do it. And they love him for it.

In the course, these entrepreneurs and CEOs in training learn that everyone, from the babysitter to the boss, has leadership qualities that can be encouraged and developed in ways that help the family and the society, as well as the business.

As a student, you're expected to do a serious personal inventory to figure out what your core values really are. Sounds easy, but it's not. Try it yourself. Sit down and make a list of what it truly important to you. Okay, that part's not too difficult. The hard part comes when you take the time to figure out which of these values you are honoring in your life right now. That's when the shock sets in. Then Stewart tells his students to think ahead fifteen years and write an analysis of what their life and values will be like. That will certainly make you wonder how well you are fulfilling your social contract right now.

I think many people who take Stewart's courses find them to be tougher than anything else they study at school. But think about it. Would you rather work for a CEO who has a good sense of himself and his place in the world, or someone who is maniacally dedicated to making money to the exclusion of everything else?

Stewart's newest book is called *Total Leadership: Be a Better Leader, Have a Richer Life,* and it focuses on making changes that are good for work, family, community and self, and realizing that you are part of something bigger than just taking care of number one. It's based on these precepts: 1) Be real. Know what's important and stick to it. 2) Be whole. Have integrity and respect for all sides of yourself and others. 3) Be innovative. Experiment and be creative, all the time.

Stewart is a hero because he doesn't advocate taking the easy way out. He supports business and knows that people want and need to make money. But he also pushes them to be better than they ever thought they could be. It's tough in this 24/7 world, where we work from our PDAs while riding in taxis. But I'm glad we've got someone influential pushing integration of business, home, and community in our lives.

This hero might just make us all a little richer in the process.

"Management is doing things right; leadership is doing the right things."

—Peter Drucker

Not all managers are in the business of making money. Take the Chinese middle school principal Ye Zhiping, for instance. He was in charge of a school of 2,323 people in Sangzao when the devastating level 8.0 earthquake rocked the region in 2008, leveling buildings, upending bridges, and crushing the life and limbs of innocent people. Ten thousand kids were buried as various schools collapsed around them. But in Ye's school, the kids dove under their desks for safety when the tremors hit, and then moved immediately outside for a head count after the earthquake subsided. Every student survived.

Parents converged on the school terrified for their children's lives. When they came face-to-face with the entire student body, it was like a miracle. No wonder the parents started calling the principal Angel Ye.

Of course, as is so often the case, this miracle was partly the result of good planning. Ye had done a heroic job of thinking toward the future and devoting his time and energy—far beyond the official requirements of his job—to making sure it was safer.

Ye always felt a responsibility toward his students that

went beyond just doing his job and collecting a paycheck. In the 1990s, he started to feel nervous about how decrepit his school was looking. That made him wonder how well it was made and whether it would hold up if there were a disaster.

The four-story building looked nice. But Ye, who had worked there for thirty years, starting as a teacher, said no government inspectors ever came to check on the concrete structure as it was being built. Ye worried that it would just disintegrate during the next quake. He wanted to fix it, but how?

We all know how bureaucracies work—they don't. And China is certainly one of the more difficult bureaucracies to negotiate. But somehow, Ye managed to get the government to cough up tens of thousands of dollars to fix his school. Ye had workers put metal rods in the concrete pillars that held up the place, and he secured the concrete floor panels so they wouldn't collapse during an earthquake.

It was amazing foresight. Since the 2008 earthquake, engineers have concluded that it was the lack of metal rods and the shaky concrete floors that made so many schools collapse that awful day.

Now mind you, Ye had no way of predicting an earthquake. All his efforts to fix the school could have gone completely unnoticed. But he went ahead and did it. The happy result was that when the earthquake hit, though it killed a thousand students in a nearby school, all of Ye's kids got out, and the building remained standing. He wasn't trying to be a hero; he was just doing what he considered his duty. Now the world admires him. And the kids he saved owe him their lives. The world could use more managers like Ye.

"Values are like fingerprints. Nobody's are the same, but you leave 'em all over everything you do."

—Elvis Presley

I love it when businesspeople apply their entrepreneurial gusto to help their communities, because the results are often successful beyond the wildest dreams of traditional nonprofit organizations. Thinking big comes naturally to Alan Graham, an Austin innovator, who made a fortune building cargo areas for airlines, among other ventures. About eight years ago, he was having lunch with a friend when the fellow mentioned a group he'd heard about in Corpus Christie that was taking hot cocoa and blankets to homeless people during the Christmas holidays.

Immediately, a lightbulb went on in Alan's head. That's how it works for entrepreneurs—their best ideas usually pop up out of the blue. The real planning goes into the execution. Anyway, his idea was to use a mobile catering truck, like those that sell meals at construction sites, to deliver hot meals to homeless men and women around Austin.

"I can't say I've ever eaten off a catering truck in my whole life, but this just came to me," Alan said.

Not long after that, he brought up the concept with some parishioners at his Catholic church, in a wealthy Austin neighborhood. He told them he thought it was a fantastic idea that could be used in all sorts of different ways around the country. Apparently they agreed, because he got promises of $25,000 in donations right there.

He was concerned that he was a bit out of touch with the homeless. So one night he and four others from his church just decided to try it. They packed up seventy-five box lunches and went out in a van with a homeless person they'd met as their guide.

"I knew it was the real deal," he said.

Thus, in 1998 Loaves and Fishes was founded, with the five guys from the church and the homeless man who had served as their liaison. From there, the service took off. They have a large food prep area. Several trucks. And these days, fifty-six-hundred people volunteer one evening a month for two hours of giving food to the homeless. At the headquarters of Loaves and Fishes there's a map marked with eighty sites where homeless people congregate in Austin. The volunteers split up into teams of six and choose a spot to begin. The only requirement is that they give away all seventy-five of their meals, which are composed of a sandwich, fruit, a drink and cookies, along with toiletries and fresh socks for anyone who needs them. There's no limit to the number of stops they make. Sometimes the new volunteers prefer to work with homeless families before they try to take on more difficult cases, like crack addicts and prostitutes. The volunteers benefit, too. There's nothing like seeing someone living on the streets to make you realize how good you have it.

It's an easy, safe way for people to volunteer. And it's a huge boon to the homeless population. Loaves and Fishes has expanded to San Antonio, New Orleans, Minnesota, Ohio, and Tennessee.

But as I said, Alan is an entrepreneur. And entrepreneurs rarely stop at just one idea. When he was staying in a recreational vehicle while on a hunting trip it occurred to him that he should create an RV park for homeless people, Habitat on Wheels. He thought it would be an inexpensive way to get them off the streets. He raised money and bought five, as a start. The plan was working well so he bought some more. The formerly homeless people pay a small rent for their trailers so it's not just charity. Alan wants to get two hundred homeless people off the streets of Austin and into their own trailers in a planned community for the homeless.

While he has a long way to go to fulfill his goals, Alan is heartened by the effect the trailers have had on a few men who live in an Austin trailer park he founded.

The men have a lot in common, having lived on the streets, and they sometimes visit each other in their small trailers. Each unit is about 250 square feet, with a double bed, couch, kitchen, and a tiny shower. They come with linens, kitchen stuff, and a TV.

"Compared to sleeping next to railroad tracks every night with the bugs and the dirt, this is a palace," Mr. Kendrick said. Nothing fancy. That's what Alan is all about. He likes things straightforward and well thought out, and his heroics have surely paid off in spades.

Ordinary People, Extraordinary Choices
You Make the Call!

You've just moved into a new apartment, and it's taking forever to unpack your boxes and put all your junk away. In fact, there's so much stuff that you feel like throwing it out the window. But that's not your dilemma. The problem is that you haven't been able to get your cable hooked up yet, so you don't have any access to the information highway. So you turn on the wireless on your laptop to see if there are any free Wi-Fi signals around. There aren't any, but you do notice that one Wi-Fi signal has the same name as your new neighbor, who just had you over for welcome-to-the-neighborhood drinks the night before. His signal is password-protected, but you decide to see if you can break it. First you try his girlfriend's name. No luck. Then you try his apartment number. Still no luck. Then you remember how much he loved his pet turtle, named Ertle. Bingo! Ertle is the password. You type it in and get online. And no one is the wiser, other than your guilty conscience.

YOU COULD:

A) Smash your computer to smithereens to atone for your bad behavior.

B) Run next door and confess to your sins and say you committed them only in the name of highlighting his security weaknesses.

C) Offer to pay him for the time were online on his dime.

D) Install your own service, and keep it password-free as a way of making up for your transgression.

Well, there's no question that hacking into someone else's service by guessing what their password is could be considered rude at best, and criminal at worst. But that doesn't mean you have to offer up a confession, and prostrate yourself before the gods of technology. Instead, think twice next time before hacking someone's password. You don't need to offer to pay him for his service, because you didn't cost him anything extra. But it might be good for your karma, and little bit heroic, to keep your own service password-free, so that the next new neighbor isn't tempted to steal.

CHAPTER TEN

Honor and Duty

Some heroes never have to answer the question, "What should I do?"

It just never comes up. They merely take care of the task.

Twenty-three-year-old Army Staff Sergeant David Price is that sort of guy. Seated in an easy chair in the Henderson, Nevada, subdivision where his mother lives, David, at first glance, looks like your average young man, albeit one who works out and has unusually good posture. But spend a few minutes with him and you'll find an intense energy beneath the calm surface that only hints at the fact that he's been through two tours of duty in Afghanistan and two in Iraq.

You see, David is an elite soldier, and our country is lucky to have him. He knows how to take a horrible situation and make it better. In one case, in particular, on a roadside outside of Baghdad where chaos threatened to take over, David's heroism paid off in a big way. However, he'd never put it that way, because while David is quick to act when he's needed, he never puts his name and the word *hero* in the same sentence.

David grew up shuttling between his mother's home in Las Vegas and his father's rural place in St. George, Utah. She's the executive director of the League Real Estate Institute at UNLV and serves on the Henderson Planning Commission. David's dad is a wildlife manager. They divorced when David was young but were committed to raising him together. It seems that their efforts paid off. He spent most of the school year with his mom and roamed the woods and desert with his dad on weekends and vacations.

"I wasn't anything exceptional," he says.

In high school he drifted and got in trouble amid the manicured xeriscapes of the Las Vegas subdivisions filled with fast-food chains and drive-through this and that, which don't offer much in the way of inspiration to a young man in search of meaning.

"Trouble in the form of alcohol, mainly," he says.

So his parents decided he should move in with his father for his junior year.

"You know, sometimes a man needs a man," he says.

St. George was a far cry from Las Vegas. And his father was stricter than his mom.

"I didn't appreciate it at the time, but looking back that was just what I needed," said David.

Soon after arriving in St. George, he decided that he wanted to be an Army Ranger. He had a sense of duty and watching the aftermath of the attacks of September 11, 2001, on TV had affected David profoundly.

"I realized for the first time that there were people like that who'd want to do us harm. I knew I'd rather see the war fought over there versus on our turf," he says.

He admits that the thought of going to war excited him. But a big part of it was that he wanted to get away from St. George, and his strict father.

Of course, there are few places on earth that are more regimented, or more liberating, than Army Ranger training. The Rangers are the Army's elite force. Fewer than 50 percent graduate from the nine-week program, which puts soldiers through a demanding, sometimes brutal, series of exercises designed to separate the wheat from the chaff and produce tough, duty-bound leaders. You've seen the Army grunts struggling over obstacle courses. You've heard of the all-night marches. The lack of sleep. The two meals a day, at most, on days that last for twenty hours and start anew with just three hours of sleep. It's exhausting. And satisfying.

"That's why you want to be there," says David. "The whole thing is very focused and challenging. The people you're next to on a daily basis are a lot saner than the average person. They are dedicated to their work. And if you get into a gunfight you'd rather be with those guys, you know?"

David has seen plenty of action, although he doesn't talk much about his experiences as a soldier. Still, when you earn a Silver Star for valor, as David did, people are going to hear your story. When I heard it, David immediately joined my pantheon.

It was May 22, 2007, and David was stationed near Taji, Iraq. That's on MSR Tampa, a road that runs the full length of Iraq, from Syria to Kuwait. The road is six lanes of desolation at the best of times and narrow lanes of terror at the worst. Insurgents hide in the desert or in farmhouses and grassy areas obscured by dust and attack military and civilian vehicles with weapons or remote-control IEDs (improvised explosive devices) cobbled together from cell phones and other devices. These remote-controlled bombs can rip up a car or tear a man's leg off. About 40 percent of American casualties in Iraq have been due to IEDs. MSR Tampa is an incredibly perilous road.

David had only been stationed at Camp Taji for a few days. The departing unit hadn't communicated well with the locals and the situation was tense. Since David and his platoon were the new guys on the block, they were more prone to making mistakes, and generally putting themselves at risk. The bad guys knew this and were taking advantage of the greenhorns.

"We're taking mortars constantly. Getting shot at, potshots all the time. You just knew there was something big going to happen. But you just didn't know when and where," said David.

"Adversity introduces a man to himself."

—Unknown

David's platoon was supposed to patrol a fifteen-kilometer stretch of the road and keep their eyes out for trouble. They were a bit undermanned and had only enough soldiers to send two to four vehicles out at a time, which was dangerous.

"But you gotta do what you gotta do," said David.

This day there were two vehicles out. David had been up all night on silent kill team (SKT), which was looking out for people setting up roadside bombs. He was sleeping in the Joint Security outpost when he got a call on the radio.

"We have a catastrophic kill on vehicle," said the voice.

He put on his gear and jumped into the truck with the other seven members of his platoon, including his platoon leader, and headed toward where the Stryker had been blown up. Strykers are light combat vehicles that you board and exit via ramps from the rear. When David and his makeshift squad arrived, his platoon leader put them right into the fray and he inadvertently parked on top of an unexploded IED just twenty yards from the smoldering Stryker they were hoping to rescue. Thank heaven the previous explosions had blown the blasting caps away from these devices.

"They would have blown our Stryker up. We should have been dead," David says.

But he didn't have very much time to think about that.

As he went down the ramp of the Stryker, they immediately encountered the enemy. The rounds were flying. He jumped into a shallow ravine next to the vehicle and five soldiers followed him.

"There were at least fifteen enemy personnel in the building and surrounding area shooting at us," says David.

David could see that insurgents were trying to get into the destroyed Stryker so they could pull the bodies out, make prisoners of the wounded, and take documents and equipment. He and his fellow soldiers fired on them to drive them away.

Things were chaotic. David stepped in to control the operation and rescue whoever was in the mangled Stryker.

"I knew a couple of them were alive 'cause I could hear 'em screaming," he said. "They were wounded and couldn't get out."

He couldn't do anything until his platoon got the upper hand. Otherwise, he'd just end up with more wounded or dead soldiers on his hands. A Stryker mounted with a 105-mm gun, called an MGS, had joined them, and it was waiting about seventy yards away for orders to fire. David looked over and said to himself, "All right, yeah, that thing needs to be shooting right now," so he radioed over to give it the target.

The MGS blasted the building the insurgents were using for cover as they fired on the American soldiers. That was step one. There was no time to think about anything but moving forward, making sure the others were protected as well as possible, and working to evacuate the bombed striker.

Already, David was going beyond the call of duty. He wasn't obligated to take command. He had no orders to risk his life. Yet he felt a responsibility—rescuing those people was his imperative. And he didn't see anyone else who could take over.

"It was kind of textbook," he says. "I knew what I needed to do and how it needed to be done."

That makes sense. But in my mind, there's a huge difference between knowing what you're supposed to do when the bullets are flying and you can see a Stryker full of injured—possibly dying—fellow soldiers, and actually doing it.

"You've just got to keep moving," says David.

David thinks pretty much anyone could be a hero, given the right situation. Especially people in the military. "Put anyone in the same situation and they'll do what I did," he says.

I know it's not true that everyone would respond the way David did. His behavior was exceptional. He doesn't want to be called a hero so I won't call him one—at least not to his face.

"So you don't want to be a big shot?" I ask him as we sit in his mom's air-conditioned home.

"Just stay under the radar. You don't want to draw too much attention," he says, petting his mom's dog.

He couldn't avoid the spotlight that day on MSR Tampa, however. Now that he'd quieted some of the enemy fire by ordering a strike on the nearby building, David had to find a way down the road to the ruined Stryker and the soldiers. About three minutes had passed since he'd jumped out of the Stryker.

He positioned two people to stay with the functioning vehicle. Then he set up three guys at the back of the downed Stryker and climbed to higher ground with a couple of other guys to keep the peace up there. All together, they formed a 360-degree perimeter.

"Before you even start messing with casualties, you got to make sure that you're safe," he said.

Then he and another guy returned to the downed Stryker and started doing "cas evac," which is Army speak for pulling out the injured. David had undergone extensive first-aid training with the Rangers. That was a good thing, because the medic on duty was new to Iraq and inexperienced with battlefield injuries. One guy in the Stryker had lost most of a leg, and David immediately started an IV with medicine that made his blood thicker to keep him from bleeding out. David was being fired on at the time.

"Just pop shots," he says, dismissively.

Still, he was frightened. But the adrenaline, and the sense of duty, kept him going. He applied a tourniquet to the amputee and then treated shrapnel wounds the man had on his face and arms. Then he pulled him from the ruined Stryker and got him to safety. There was still more to do. Risking his life, but trusting his men to keep him safe, David returned to the vehicle and removed the other wounded and terrified soldiers. Finally, he removed two dead soldiers, because you never leave a soldier behind.

Then he directed his troops to fire on the remaining insurgents. They drove them out of the area. Helicopters landed to take the dead and wounded away. Then he and his men, along with some new arrivals, pushed a hundred yards into town and set up a post on high ground. The end of another day in Iraq.

"A hero is an ordinary individual who finds the strength to persevere and endure in spite of overwhelming obstacles."

—Christopher Reeve

The Army awarded David the Silver Star for gallantry in action, which is one of the country's highest military honors. David says he's proud of the medal. But it's a bittersweet honor because others had to die for him to get it. His mom has it now.

"Who are your heroes, David?" I ask him.

"My parents," he says. "They raised me right."

I have a feeling that David and another soldier, Marine Sergeant Merlin German, would have understood each other well. Merlin grew up the youngest of eight children in Westchester, north of New York City. His bedroom was decorated with New York Yankees paraphernalia, pictures from the gangster flick *Scarface,* model cars, and hip-hop posters.

He was a big kid, intimidating in some ways. But his

brother Ariel says that while Merlin could sometimes be a bully, he was also known as a joker who kept people entertained, someone who'd help other kids at the drop of a hat. He was.

He didn't have a date for his senior prom but told a school counselor he didn't mind, he'd just dance with someone else's date. And his dance card was packed all night long.

He and his siblings were forbidden to play with toy guns when they were growing up and he decided he wanted to be a soldier some day so he could shoot a real one. He enlisted in the Marine Corps after high school.

He was posted to Iraq in 2005 and became known among his fellow marines for being good at spotting hidden explosives. He'd already bought a ticket for a flight home in two weeks when a roadside IED blew up Merlin's Humvee. Over 97 percent of his body was burned in the fire. He lost fingers and toes and his handsome countenance was disfigured. He was alive, but barely.

Doctors in Iraq set the goal of getting him back to the States so he could live long enough for his family to say goodbye. Merlin wound up in Brooke Army Medical Center in San Antonio, where he was given a 3 percent chance of survival. At first, he felt hopeless. His brother Ariel was shocked when he saw him because only his toes stuck out from the bandages that enveloped his entire body.

"Is that my brother?" Ariel had to ask.

Doctors covered his wounds with artificial skin, and even

tissue from cadavers. What little healthy skin remained on his body was harvested and sent to a laboratory that specialized in growing human skin. The doctors used those pieces to repair sensitive burned areas and had to suspend his arms and legs from metal bars until they healed. The doctors and nurse talked about him at their morning meetings. As the days passed, so did their prognosis on Merlin. They'd all thought he wouldn't make it. But he was showing them otherwise.

In the early months of his recovery, Merlin was depressed and hopeless at times, as any of us would be. He feared that he was so disfigured that no woman would ever be able to love him. He told people he wanted to give up. But he maintained a positive attitude. He learned to breathe on his own, without a machine to help him, and he began talking again. And he took his first steps.

The hospital staff took to calling him the "Miracle Man."

Because he was so enthusiastic about his recovery, the staff naturally turned to him to cheer up and motivate other burn patients. Kids, especially, felt a connection to Merlin. After seventeen months in the hospital, Merlin was able to move into his own apartment, with his mother and father. His mother had come to San Antonio vowing never to leave his side again. She helped him get to all his hospital appointments—he had approximately 120 surgeries in three years—and took care of him at home.

He started to dream about his future. He thought he might go to college, start a business, become a writer, or even join the

FBI. Through all his physical and emotional pain, he retained an almost magical ability to help others, especially other burn victims. They'd take one look at him and know that he understood their pain.

Merlin was so disfigured by his burns and surgeries that he feared he would frighten people who saw him on the street. And, in truth, he probably did sometimes. He used his humor and big personality to charm them. But he also knew intimately how much other burn victims suffered because of their changed appearances, and other problems.

He decided to create a foundation to help other young people who had suffered serious burns. He envisioned it as a place where people could turn for help buying an air conditioner—the heat can be incredibly oppressive to burn victims—or send them on a trip. He named it Merlin's Miracles.

While he was still in the hospital, he came up with a T-shirt that read on the front, "Got 3% chance of living . . . Q. What you gonna do?" On the back were the multiple-choice answers: "A) Fight Through, B) Stay Strong, C) Overcome Because I Am a Warrior, D) All of the Above." Of course, "D" was his answer. His foundation now sells the shirts online at merlinsmiracles.com.

Three years after returning home from Iraq, Merlin went to the hospital for surgery on his lip. It was supposed to be simpler than the 120 other surgeries he'd previously gone through. But something happened to his respiratory system—no one is quite sure, although perhaps it was just that Merlin's body couldn't handle any more trauma—and he died. This young hero was just twenty-two years old. But he lives on in Merlin's Miracles, and in the lives of many young burn victims who still turn to Merlin for inspiration. The doctors always said that Merlin beat the incredible odds against him mainly because his spirit was so strong. And now that spirit lives on. The hero endures.

"If your actions inspire others to dream more, learn more, do more and become more, you are a leader."

—John Quincy Adams

Part of the Florence Nightingale vow recited by nurses is *I will devote myself to the welfare of those committed to my care.* Following Hurricane Katrina, a nurse named Gail Gibson fulfilled this pledge in unexpected ways. I first read about Gail in *Time* magazine, and the more I looked into her story, the more amazed I was.

Gail worked in the pediatric ward of University Hospital in New Orleans and as the floodwaters rose, and hundreds of thousands of people fled the area, she realized she had no choice but to stay put. There were several dozen sickly preemies under her care, and she couldn't just leave them to the floodwaters. Almost everyone else in the hospital had fled when the levees broke, although other nurses also stayed to help.

When the electricity went out, Gail and her nurses relied

on a generator. When that was flooded out, they had no lights and could only communicate with the outside world via ham radio. No electricity meant no incubators or respirators, and many of the babies were so weak that Gail and the other nurses had to hold them in their arms to keep them warm.

The days passed. Gail felt incredibly isolated and frightened. But the kids needed her. One day a helicopter sent word that it would rescue the babies from a high spot at Tulane University, just a few blocks away. Gail organized the nurses into rowboats to carry the preemies to the helicopter, but it never arrived. As they rowed back to the hospitals with the delicate babies, the nurses were so drained that some weren't sure they could continue. Many of Gail's staffers were crying and upset, so she walked through the ward encouraging them to keep strong and remember to put their preemies first, always. Gibson herself barely slept. But the problems continued to grow. As the days passed, she took on the duty of overseeing nurses in other parts of the hospital. And, amazingly, a new preemie was born, just twenty-three weeks old, in the hospital during this time. When, after five days, the hospital was evacuated, all the preemies were still healthy and strong.

Thanks to the tenacity and heroic efforts of Gail and her nurses, twenty-six little New Orleans residents—plus one— were ready to grow along with their damaged city. Let's hope that some of those preemies grow into heroes themselves.

Ordinary People,
Extraordinary Choices
You Make the Call!

After two back-to-back shifts walking the streets of downtown Los Angeles, you're ready to take off your badge, get in your car, and head back to the suburbs for a swim and a good night's sleep. As you pull onto the 110 Freeway entrance ramp, the traffic jams up. The guy ahead jumps out of his car and starts screaming. You look up and there's a man hanging from the edge of the freeway overpass, looking like he's drugged out of his mind. You can't believe it. After sixteen hours on the job you've got to run into this? You look in the rearview and see there's room to back up and go down a side street.

YOU COULD:

A) Escape down the side street and pick up the freeway at the next entrance. After all, there are plenty of on-duty cops in L.A.

B) Call one of your buddies who is on duty.

C) Sit and watch the scene unfold, to make sure nothing too terrible happens.

D) Put your badge back on, get out, and save the guy's life.

I think most cops would choose D. It's just part and parcel of taking the policeman's oath and doing your duty. It's also the riskiest and most uncomfortable choice. Sure, some people would choose A, feeling they're entitled to a break. And B might help somewhat. But acting on choice C, when you're capable and strong, would be a crime. D is clearly the only choice in this situation, and it's one I hope we would all make.

CHAPTER ELEVEN

Spanning Borders

Some heroes must cross borders to help others. These borders might divide countries, societies, or states of mind. And I've followed these heroes to some strange and forbidding places to share their stories with the world.

On a visit to Bogota, Colombia, in 1990, I saw a group of what appeared to be homeless kids climbing down into some manholes in the middle of a beautiful downtown avenue. With a bit of trepidation, I decided to follow them down into a fetid sewer and came face to face with the underground world of the "gamines," or street urchins: boys and girls whose only refuge is the rivers of waste underneath the streets of the capital city.

These days Bogota is a model city, with bikeways and eco-mass transit and lovely streets. But in 1990 there was plenty to fear in this city at the northern tip of the Andes mountains in South America. The city of seven million people is a literally breathtaking 8,661 feet above sea level, making it the third-highest city in the world. And walking the streets of Bogota, you feel as if you are in the clouds. The skies are often gray and the air, while rarely freezing, doesn't usually get much above 75 degrees. People in Bogota have the serious nature I associate with New Yorkers. And like them, they tend to dress in dark colors: black slacks, leather shoes, dark blue V-neck sweaters below charcoal sport jackets. Bogota is a city of shadows.

On the one hand, it is among the most sophisticated cities in the world, with an amazing array of writers, artists, businesspeople, and others employed by universities, factories, and small businesses. On the other hand, the city, as well as the country of Colombia, has a history of violence that is astounding.

There was the war of a thousand days that began in 1899 over a dispute between the Conservative and Liberal parties. It lasted three years and spread murder, dismemberment, and mayhem to every corner of the country, which at the time included the isthmus we call Panama. It ended three years later leaving behind total economic ruin. Then there was La Violencia, or, The Violence. This war began in 1948 when the presidential candidate for the Liberal Party was murdered. This sparked a second war between the Conservative and Liberal parties that lasted ten years and cost 300,000 or so lives.

The brutality was hard to believe. Most killings were done with knives, bludgeons, and machetes, and after a time the violence became so systemic that, in rural areas, families attacked each other without really knowing why. Corpses were marked with mutilations, such as the "undershirt cut," in which the victim's arms and head were cut off, the "necktie cut," where the tongue was cut out and set on the chest, and the "flower vase cut," where the arms and legs were cut off and inserted into the splayed torso like a flower arrangement.

I tell you this, not to shock you, but to illustrate one awful aspect of Colombian culture that continues to influence the country. Millions of people fled their homes during La Violencia.

In the 1960s, left-wing guerrillas inspired by Castro, Mao, and others rose up against the government. Predictably, right-wingers formed paramilitary groups to "deal" with the guerrillas. The paramilitary groups were, basically, roving death squads meant to "clean up" society. A trend that increased with the advent of the drug trade. Violence in Colombia grew proportionately along with the worldwide demand for cocaine. And, of course, the leftist guerrillas used some of the drug profits to fuel their battles.

By the late 1980s, Colombia was one of the most dangerous countries on earth. There were narcotraficantes shooting each other, paramilitaries killing whomever they didn't like, and street criminals running wild. By 1990, there were about five thousand murders a year in Bogota. Wealthy people would travel to and from the airport in jeeps manned by security guards carrying automatic weapons. Bombs were common. The newspapers were filled with photographs of corpses and of tables with piles and piles of seized kilo packages of pure cocaine. The murder rate was the highest in the world.

As the violence continued, people became cynical and no longer trusted judges and police to keep them safe. No one expected any help from government social services. The country became lawless. They turned to do-it-yourself justice in the form of paramilitaries.

That left the homeless kids virtually defenseless, shunned by society, and ignored by government officials.

⁂

As the cities in Colombia grew over the years, with people fleeing violence, poverty, and neglect, hoping to find new lives in metropolises like Bogota, the homeless situation just got worse. Many of the rural people were poorly educated, with few skills that would help them get by in the city, let alone fulfill their dreams of getting richer.

By 1990, the increased urban poverty had brought the local governments to the point of giving up on them. Nothing anyone did was enough. The poverty just grew. Families couldn't get by. Instead, they'd often just break apart. Bogota had about 14,000 people living in its streets. Most had been homeless for years. Over half said they were on the street due to family problems.

Kids lost their parents to violence or poverty. There was no safety net. Children ended up on the street, subsisting on nothing but prayers. Once on the street, the kids had to learn quickly how to care for themselves. Unfortunately, a lot of them learned how to sell their bodies, inhale cocaine, and steal.

At the time, Bogota had more homeless people than Mexico City or anywhere else in Latin America. Walking the streets at night, you stepped through fields of homeless children sleeping on the sidewalks or sitting on low walls, their crusty skin and matted hair giving them a feral look. The acrid smell of glue they sniffed and the bazuko, or cheap cocaine residue, that they smoked filled the night sky on some blocks as these kids numbed themselves with the toxic smoke.

That also meant you had to watch your wallet; these gamines were crafty little thieves. "Good" citizens didn't want to have to deal with hungry, dirty urchins stealing, begging, and using the streets as a toilet. The Colombian authorities responded with violence in the form of a "rehabilitation campaign," which drove hundreds of these kids into the sewers beneath the streets of Bogota to escape the harsh world above.

Most everyone ignored these kids. What with the violence, inflation, corruption, drugs, and just the difficulties of day-to-day living, people were glad when they disappeared.

Fortunately, someone else was more interested: an unlikely hero I met hanging around near the entrance to one of the sewers. His name was Jaime Jaramillo, and he would become my guide into the gamines' hell on earth.

It was dark down there, with a constant flow of water between my feet. Damp. Rats as big as cats scurrying out of my path. The smell of human waste permeated the air. I immediately wanted to leave.

"Jaime Jaramillo!" my guide called out to let the gamines know that it was him and not someone with evil intent invading their dank turf.

Jaime was a petroleum geologist making a quarter of a million dollars a year identifying oil fields for international petroleum companies when he saw something that was to change his life forever.

It was December 1973, and Jaime was driving down a road when he saw a young homeless girl run into the street to pick up the box of a toy doll that someone had thrown out of their car. As the little girl tried to grab the box, a truck struck her and killed her.

It turned out that the box she gave her life for was empty: there was no doll. Jaime realized that homeless children had become just another part of the urban scenery, unnoticed and uncared for. He couldn't let that continue. When he heard about the sewer kids, he decided to work with them.

And here, coming out of the long dark tunnel, were some of the forgotten kids he was dedicated to helping. First came a girl of sixteen, pretty, smart looking, and two months pregnant. Sandra lived with her boyfriend Juan in a large hole on the side of the sewer. As long as the canal of waste didn't rise up a few feet, as it sometimes did after a heavy rain, Juan and Sandra would be okay. They had lived in the hole for more than a year.

In a country like Colombia, with so many problems, at the time it seemed the entire population became totally indifferent. The death squad industry was thriving in Colombia. Some of these squads were political in nature, killing as a way of gaining power. Others had a self-defined social mission: to cleanse society of its filth, with a "limpieza social." Where better to find this filth than in the sewers.

The death squads were made up of regular citizens—police, grocery store owners, businesspeople—fed up with crime who felt they had no other way to control it. Colombians have always tended to turn to "private justice" when the government fails them. Of course, the squads also drew psychos. They'd kill at night with guns, knives, machetes, whatever, and leave bodies in the street as a message. Between 1988 and 1993, they killed nearly two thousand people. About 125 of them were gamines.

One homeless kid described three times when he was almost killed by social cleansers. Twice he was sleeping on the street when a policeman drove by on a motorcycle and fired shots at him. Another time a black BMW pulled up and shot him and his girlfriend as they smoked bazuko on a sidewalk. His girlfriend was killed. He said he'd been picked up by the police, who took him to the station and tortured him by forcing his head underwater, beating him with a stick, and attaching wires to his testicles and giving him electrical shocks.

No wonder these kids retreat to the sewers to escape the violence above.

The sewers were safer because cops and death squads were unlikely to follow them into these narrow, dark passageways.

Of course, that was before the cops and paramilitaries started setting the sewer kids on fire.

You can take a jar of gas and empty it into the sewer, drop in a flaming rag, and then close the manhole cover to let the kids barbecue. Police officers had been known to joke that this was a good rehabilitation technique for thieves: Once they burned to death, they'll never steal again. When they aren't burning the kids, they'll just terrify them. They'll burn their clothes. They'll beat them up. Or worse. Hundreds of kids in Bogota—no one knows exactly how many—have simply disappeared, part of what the Colombian military calls its "cleanup campaign."

Jaime sometimes felt like he was the only person in all of Bogota who cared what happened to these kids. And so, when the sun goes down in this city of seven million, Jaime can be found collecting the food and clothing, which he distributes to the children. He ventures into the sewers alone, wearing a wetsuit in case he falls into high water, and carrying a first-aid kit to help mend any injuries the kids have.

Jaime soon realized that just giving the kids food and medicine wasn't going to make a lasting difference in their lives.

To accomplish something larger and more enduring, he established a foundation called Fundación Niños de los Andes (www.ninandes.org) to help them. The foundation built three houses for the homeless kids and when I visited, three hundred former street kids were receiving free meals, clothing, health care, and an education. Half of the foundation's expenses were paid for by private donations. The other half came out of Jaime's pocket. He saw the kids as part of his extended family. I met some of the ones he'd helped. Like Claudia, an eleven-year-old girl who was born with Down syndrome. Her family used her as a mule to carry tanks of hot water on her back. The water leaked, causing third-degree burns that still scarred her. Then Jaime took me over to meet a baby who had been born in the sewer to parents who were drug addicts. To quiet his cries they had the baby sniff glue. Then there was Andres, a thirteen-year-old boy who had spent most of his life in the sewers. He was addicted to cocaine and glue when Jaime first met him. Now he's a good student, and a great kid, living at the foundation.

Jaime's assistance doesn't end with the food, the clothing, a home, and an education. He also helps the kids become productive adults . . . training them and then finding them jobs in all kinds of professions.

I couldn't help wondering about the parents of these children. Did they ever think of them? Did they ever wonder how they were faring in the harsh world of Bogota? Had they forgotten that they, too, were children once?

The parents might have forgotten, but not Jaime Jaramillo, the hero of the sewers.

"There is no higher religion than human service.
To work for the common good is the greatest creed."

—Woodrow Wilson

A short flight across the Caribbean Sea on the island of Hispaniola, I met another heroic man in a land devastated by poverty and violence. Father Edwin Paraison is an Episcopal priest from Haiti who has risked his life numerous times to rescue children being held as virtual slaves across the border in the Dominican Republic.

These two countries share an island and both have a history of despotic rulers who maintain control through brute force. But their respective cultures couldn't be more different. Haiti was a French colony. The vast majority of its people are dark-skinned descendants of slaves, and their common language is a French patois called Creole. Haiti is the poorest country in the Western Hemisphere. In 1991, when I visited the island, the average wage was just $300 a year. More than half the people struggle to get just one meal a day. Life expectancy in Haiti was just fifty-three years.

The Dominican Republic, on the other hand, had a life expectancy of sixty-seven years. It was a Spanish colony, and its descendants are generally lighter skinned. There was extreme poverty but not nearly as desperate as Haiti. Dominicans speak Spanish. They often rely on Haitians to do their manual labor. It's not surprising that they look down on the Haitians, and often treat them no better than animals.

Born in Haiti in 1962, Father Edwin went on to study at a seminary for Episcopal priests. Fortunately, for the sugarcane kids who would later see him as a hero, his first posting was at a church in a town called La Romana, in the Dominican Republic. This town is located in one of the most desirable tourism areas of the DR, with luxurious resorts such as Casa de Campo and Altos de Chavon. Wealthy and influential people like Oscar del la Renta own second homes here amid the lush tropical countryside. For many, it's a wonderful place to golf, dance to merengue, or lie by the pool. For others, it's not so great.

La Romana has always been a company town, meaning it was created to serve the sugar companies that harvest cane in the area. There are plenty of poor people in the DR but not enough, it seems, to satisfy the need for cane cutters. It's said that Dominicans just won't do the work, because cutting cane is one of the most dangerous and brutal jobs on earth.

Sugarcane matures at a height of anywhere from six to eighteen feet. And since the cane is a grass, it constantly sends up fresh, razor-sharp shoots. The leaves, too, have sharp needles that lodge in the workers' skin. Often the fields are burned before harvest to knock out the weeds and make the cane easier to cut. Wading into a smoldering field with a machete is like entering hell on earth. The sun beats down and sharply pointed stalks are like spears that can easily gouge a cutter's eyes out.

Days start at dawn and end after sunset. The cutter passes through the mucky fields, stooping low to cut through the two-inch-thick stalk near its base. Holding the stalk in one hand, he straightens up and whacks off the top, including the leaves, and tosses the clean section into a pile. Sweating profusely in the hot fields, the workers often lose control of their machetes and cut their feet open.

Each worker chops thousands of stalks a day in a numbing repetition of bending, chopping, and stacking. They cut for two days and then spend the third day loading the cane onto oxcarts that take it to the weigh station.

In rich countries, cutters usually wear protective shields on their wrists and long sleeves so they won't be sliced by the sharp cane. But the Haitian cutters in the DR just work with whatever clothes they can scrounge up, and often they look like they are dressed in rags held together by grime. Many of them are teenage boys or even younger, and are considered second-class citizens in the DR, with few rights.

No wonder Father Paraison felt compelled to help them.

The sugarcane plantations in the DR cover thousands of square miles. Each year they send 300,000 metric tons of the sweet stuff north to the United States, and get about $200 million in return. Most of the plantations are owned by the government and plenty of people profit along the way, as sugar travels from the cane field to your bowl of breakfast cereal. But the slave boys who cut the cane get only a bitter harvest of misery and a hopeless future. Some of them are as young as eight years old and work twelve hours a day. I met an eight-year-old boy who had been working the fields for half of his young life.

He was hungry and thin, wearing a dirty blue T-shirt that hung loosely over his emaciated body. That's what happens when you are kidnapped from your country and sold to the Dominican Armed Forces for $12, as Horacio alleges happened. Slavery, it appeared, was alive and well in the Dominican Republic.

According to international human rights groups, at the time hundreds of children were being sold at Haitian border towns like Jimani. The common wisdom said they were being purchased by military officials who passed them on to the plantations. The workers said they were beaten with the butts of shotguns and treated like animals. The Dominicans called them *braceros*, or laborers, a term that has a special resonance for me. That's the word the Anglos used to describe Mexicans who were brought north to man U.S. factories early in the twentieth century.

About thirty thousand Haitians worked in the fields. No one knew the exact number because these laborers were undocumented. Technically, they did not exist. A few people have tried to organize them into unions without success. The last two who tried were assassinated as they worked in a field.

Most of the cane cutters signed up for work with *buscones*, or recruiters, at the bus station in Port au Prince, Haiti. They rode the colorful little Haitian "top top" buses to the border of the Dominican Republic, hoping for a better life. It was a sham. The buscones never told them they were going to work in the fields.

Most of the children the buscone recruits were abandoned by their parents and, once they get across the border, they lose touch with everyone back in Haiti.

Their new home was usually a one-room shack shared with seven or eight other people. No electricity, running water, or bathrooms. They got very little food. In fact, most of them just chewed on sugarcane for the energy to cut more.

You might wonder, "Why didn't these children complain or, run away?" The answer? Sugarcane fields are controlled by guards, or foremen, on horseback carrying shotguns and pistols.

The day started before the sun came up and often ended after nightfall. All the braceros I spoke with were covered with cuts and bruises, and some had lost fingers to machetes and eyes to stalks of cane.

To keep the workers on the plantation, the government paid them with vouchers they could use to buy food at company stores. A week's work bought maybe a pound of fish, some beans, rice, and cooking oil.

Sometimes it seemed like Father Paraison was the only person who cared. Working on a weekly budget that probably wouldn't buy lunch at a good New York restaurant, Father

Paraison risked his life to smuggle kids out of the plantations and back into Haiti. Sometimes he'd give the guards rum to keep them quiet. Other times he'd just risk it.

I went along on one trip where he drove his rattling old pickup truck into the cane fields to one of the pathetic bateys. There he called for the Haitian children working the fields to come with him. He wouldn't take adults, because he didn't have the facilities to help them, and he couldn't save everyone. Boys ran to the pickup, five, ten, twenty of them, and more came until there were about thirty boys riding in the back of the truck. Father Paraison beamed, nervously. He knew the fields were full of armed men on horseback who wouldn't think twice about using violence to secure their workers. And he knew that he was just a Haitian animal himself in their eyes. But he did the right thing. So far, that year, he had rescued eighty kids, taking them across the border and giving them bus fare back to Port au Prince.

As the pickup moved slowly along the rutted road, headed for the border of Haiti, and liberation for these kids, they broke into the chorus of freedom, singing in Creole. It was a chorus for a hero.

Ordinary People, Extraordinary Choices
You Make the Call!

You've gone down to Big Bend National Park in Texas to camp for a while with your buddies. There, amid the mountain views, the bears that come out at sunset, and the hot desert trails, you've found some peace of mind that your job had lately taken away. On the last night of your trip, you and your buddies decide to walk across the border to drink Mexican beer and have some tacos from one of the fantastic street vendors. You cross the bridge with no problem, but you notice that security is tighter these days, and you see a line of Mexicans waiting to get approval to enter the United States. Strange, you think, but that's the way of America these days. The carne adobo in the tacos was amazing, and the beers are starting to wear off when you cross back into the U.S. But you see a strange sight just upstream: a woman who looks like she might be Mexican is pointing dramatically to the center of the shallow river. There's a man there doubled over under the weight of a backpack. He's having trouble crossing. You're afraid he's going to drown. Clearly, the couple is trying to cross the river illegally.

YOU COULD:

A) Go back onto the Mexican side of the bridge and try to make your way over to the part of the river where the man is, and drag him to shore, leaving his wife safe on the other side.

B) Cross into the U.S. and try to save them from there.

C) Leave international relations to the experts, and head back to your campsite to sleep off the tacos.

D) Tell the Mexican immigration officers, or the guys from U.S. Homeland Security what's happening, and leave it to them.

This is an everyday crisis for Latinos trying to cross the border illegally into the U.S. to find work to support their families in Mexico and elsewhere in Latin America. And more and more, immigrants from other countries such as China and Russia also cross at the Mexican border. It's a heart-wrenching journey for these people, and my heart goes out to them, but I'm afraid that choices A and B are just too risky. You could face criminal sanction on top of the risk of drowning. And heroes must weigh these risks. Especially when there are options. Answer D is the best, most heroic response, and I'd suggest rushing over to whichever side, Mexican or American, is closest, and letting them initiate the rescue. Of course, if for some reason they refuse, then clearly you must step in.

CHAPTER TWELVE

Natural Heroism

S ometimes heroism starts small but has a huge effect. It all depends on whether you see a difficult situation as an opportunity to do good or as a risk that's not worth taking. Each of us can choose to do the right thing and, if it weren't for countless small acts of heroism, our society would be a sad place indeed.

One of the most extraordinary everyday heroes I've come across was a man named David Karnes. Dave was working at his desk at Deloitte Touche Tohmatsu auditors in Wilton, Connecticut, on September 11, 2001, when he made a decision that reverberated around the globe. Karnes, age fifty, had spent twenty-three years in the U.S. Marines, retiring as a staff sergeant. After seeing the televised results of the terrorist attack on the World Trade Center, he sat at his desk and prayed for God's guidance as to what he should do. At one point, he turned to his office mates and said, "You guys may not realize it but we're at war right now."

I first heard of Dave in a *Slate* magazine profile written by Rebecca Liss, and I was immediately drawn to his heroism. He wasn't a brash guy looking for adventure. He wasn't a robotic soldier. His faith in God was genuine and profound. First, he reflected, then he prepared himself, and then he acted, not knowing at all what he was getting into.

Dave left his office and drove to a church where he asked the pastor to pray to God to lead him to survivors in the rubble. He went to the barber and got a short Marine haircut before going home to don his Marine camo fatigues, which he still kept in his closet. Then he gathered some equipment, such as ropes and crampons, a flashlight and a knife that he thought might help him in whatever task he might face. He'd decided to go to the World Trade Center site and see what he could do to help.

He hopped into his Porsche, with the top down so that any police or military officials at checkpoints would see that he was a Marine, and drove down to New York City, topping out at 120 miles per hour under the intensely blue, late summer sky. On that fateful day, it was not lost on Dave that he was driving a Porsche 911.

He breezed through the barricades and made it into Manhattan. Driving downtown, he was shocked by how quickly the city had become a place under siege: few cars, stores closed, streets filled with desperate, tired people heading north, away from the thick smoke that rose from the rubble and filled the air for miles with the acrid smell of burnt rubber. He arrived at the site in the late afternoon, just after building seven fell. He left his car and moved to the edge of "the pile," as the burning ruins came to be called. The rescue operation had been aborted until the city could figure out whether or not it was safe enough for the rescuers to walk on the debris, and he saw no one. He felt very much alone. Then, as if by magic, another marine appeared dressed in camouflage. He said he was Sergeant Thomas; Dave never discovered his first name. But they immediately bonded as marines with a mission.

There were buildings on fire all around and officials were blocking people from entering the wreckage. But the two marines wanted to get inside. They couldn't see the actual ruins because of the thick black smoke. Then, just as the sun began to set, a patch of clear air revealed the devastation. The two men ran into the pile, pulling themselves over tangled steel and concrete. They were the only ones there. There was an eerie silence about the place, even with the sound of the fires.

The two heroes crawled over the debris shouting, "United States Marines. If you can hear us, yell or tap!"

The silence continued. But as he walked, Dave had a feeling there were people beneath him who needed to be saved. He continued his search.

Then he heard a faint voice in the distance. He concentrated.

"We're over here," the voice said.

He followed the sound until he found a passage descending into the debris. Dave climbed down as far as he could into the wreckage and still couldn't see anyone. But he could hear them. Two voices now. Down there, clearly, were at least two people alive. Sergeant Thomas went off to look for help.

"Don't leave us," said one of the buried men.

And Dave didn't. It had been over nine hours since the buildings collapsed. The men under the rubble were two policemen who had been in the Trade Center helping people when the world collapsed around them. They tried to keep their cool even though they were pinned under debris, unable to move. One officer, Will Jimeno, had chunks of concrete on his arms and chest, and concrete blocks on one leg. The other, Sergeant John McLoughlin, was buried even deeper in the rubble. Neither officer could move, although they could talk to each other in the depths.

Early on, before Staff Sergeant Karnes arrived, a voice had called to them from above. They answered, thinking they'd be rescued. But the voice quieted, and they never heard another word from the man. They'd been underground for hours now. It was hard to breathe and they had no idea when, or if, they'd be pulled to safety. Occasionally, fireballs would fall from above and shoot through the debris. At one point, gunshots went off underground, the bullets ricocheting off metal with lethal pings. Jimeno cringed. The policemen figured it was a dead officer's gun hit by a fireball, which caused it to shoot. Somehow, these two men were spared the bullets.

Jimeno's wife was expecting a child. He prayed to God to let him see his baby.

Between them, the men had no tools, really. Jimeno had a pair of handcuffs he'd bought when he worked as a security guard years before. He got them off his belt and tried digging his way out with these, to no avail. He dropped the cuffs. The sun went down.

Then, like a godsend, the voice rang out, "United States Marines. If you can hear us, yell or tap."

Jimeno woke up. It was Dave. When he realized someone was underground, he called his wife in Connecticut and his sister in Pittsburgh and asked them to work the phones for him. The phone system in New York was largely out of service and he didn't want to waste time trying to get through to the local police himself.

Soon, an ex-paramedic with an expired license showed up wearing his old uniform. Then came two New York City police officers from the Emergency Service Unit. All these guys crawled down into the hole with Dave. They started digging.

Dave's sister reached the Pittsburgh police, who got through to the New York police and fire departments, and soon there were more people up top offering advice and en-couragement.

There was so little room that when one of them found Jimeno's handcuffs, he tried using them as a shovel because the real shovel was too large for the space. They spent three hours digging through the precarious debris, fearing that it would collapse and kill not only those who needed rescue, but the rescuers themselves. At the surface, firefighters were shouting at them to hurry because they feared a nearby building was about to collapse.

At 11 p.m., they freed officer Jimeno. They pulled him out in a basket. At the surface, a hundred officers and firemen and other rescuers lined up and passed the basket hand by hand through the black smoke, over the debris, to a waiting ambulance. It took eight more hours to free Sergeant McLoughlin, but he, too, made it out alive.

I'm certain that if Dave hadn't driven down from Connecticut, these two policemen would be dead. The rescue efforts had been put on hold. The two marines broke the rules by following their consciences and the result was miraculous. Only twelve people were pulled alive from the rubble of the September 11 attack on the World Trade Center. Officer Jimeno and Sergeant McLoughlin were the last two people to be saved.

Dave went to the hospital with Jimeno and fell asleep on an empty bed in the psychiatric ward. During the night, someone on the hospital staff cleaned and pressed his uniform. He returned to the pile and spent nine long days doing rescue work before returning to Connecticut.

He made a few newspapers and a couple of TV shows, as a background player in the heroics of 9/11. But he never sought the limelight. Even when Hollywood put a version of his story in a movie about 9/11, he bowed out. He's an unsung hero. Well, I'd like to hum a few bars for him. Dave Karnes, a true American hero.

As for Sergeant Thomas, he just disappeared. He's never come forward, even after Dave's story made some national papers. No one knows his first name. Another hero. He did what he did, obviously, without expecting any reward other the knowledge that he contributed.

"A nation, as a society, forms a moral person, and every member of it is personally responsible for his society."

—Thomas Jefferson

Most of us know Iwo Jima as the scene of the iconic photograph, "Raising the Flag on Iwo Jima," taken by Joe Rosenthal. Sadly, few people these days know much about the brave marines who fought so fiercely to take the island. Thankfully, there's a San Antonio neurosurgeon, David Jimenez, who understands the heroism displayed every moment of that gruesome battle. Almost by accident, he took a trip to Iwo Jima and, given the chance, he did the right thing. It was a small act of kindness that reverberates through history and brings honor to men who deserve as much as they can get.

Dr. Jimenez is a fifty-four-year-old neurosurgeon who treats veterans returning from Iraq and Afghanistan. He never served in the military, so in 2007 he was invited by the secretary of defense to join a weeklong Joint Civilian Orientation Conference program for about forty civilians with little or no previous military experience. The government hoped to help these people learn more about the culture of the armed forces. When the group took a flight from Okinawa to tour Iwo Jima, Dr. Jimenez thought he'd be visiting a memorial that was well trafficked by tourists, along the lines of the memorials that dot Washington, D.C., or the Alamo in his hometown of San Antonio. But when the plane descended to a small volcanic island far from anywhere, with few signs of people living on it, he realized he was in for something different.

Iwo Jima is called a "sulfur island" because of the volcanic activity below its surface. The eight-square-mile island 650 miles south of Tokyo has thick, soft volcanic sand beaches and a 550-foot high dormant volcano called Mount Suribachi rising up from its flat surface. Before World War II, there were about a thousand people living there who got mail once a month from a ship. They mined sulfur, harvested sugarcane, and fished. The Japanese Imperial Navy kept a garrison at one end of Iwo Jima.

The island could have continued as an isolated settlement had it not been for the horrors of World War II. All the families were evacuated from Iwo Jima in 1944 when the Japanese military decided to build up their forces on the island to repel what they figured was an imminent U.S. and Allied forces invasion. No civilians have settled there since.

The Japanese airbase on the island was getting in the way of U.S. bombing missions to Tokyo when the U.S. Marines landed on those soft sands back in February 1945, hoping to neutralize the island and make it useful for a potential invasion of the Japanese mainland. Over twenty-one thousand Japanese soldiers were on the island, living in vast bunkers and eleven miles of hot tunnels that had been dug into the steaming volcanic soil.

When the first of thirty thousand marines landed on the barren beaches in the initial invasion, they were shocked to find how fierce the surf was and how far they sank into the incredibly soft volcanic sand. Each marine was carrying a heavy pack, and weapons, and as they leapt into the surf, they sank into the sand up to their knees. Climbing out was a brutal slog.

But they were more shocked by the absolute silence that greeted them. Some thought the heavy American naval and air bombardment had knocked out the Japanese. But the truth was that fortified Japanese bunkers withstood the attack, and the Japanese troops were biding their time waiting for the beaches to fill with soldiers.

Only later did the Japanese open fire in a devastating wave that killed row after row of marines. But the marines persisted. By nightfall, there were thirty thousand of them on the island and forty thousand more followed before the battle ended.

They spent hours in the sand, dodging artillery and bullets and inching their way forward. The sand of Iwo Jima remains an iconic symbol of hardship and toughness in the face of a brutal enemy. For the marines, there's almost nothing more important than this battle, and the memory of those sands.

The marines and allied forces won, prevailed, with nearly seven thousand dead and over twenty-seven thousand casualties. Only three thousand or so Japanese survived the five-week battle. Most of them hid in the tunnels. Some committed suicide. Others stayed in hiding, making night runs to get food. Gradually, they surrendered and were shocked to discover that the marines treated them with respect and gave them cigarettes or coffee. The final two stragglers didn't come out of the caves for another five years. After that, the United States administered Iwo Jima until 1968, when they gave it back to Japan.

The island that Dr. Jimenez landed on had been turned into a sedate memorial, with few people living there amid a few historic markers and functional buildings. Tourists were rare.

"Prior to arriving in Iwo Jima, my connection to the place was tenuous—mainly from watching war movies and reading history books," said Dr. Jimenez. "Before we landed, I thought it would be like Pearl Harbor, with lines of tourists and people selling paraphernalia."

He wasn't expecting to be overwhelmed. And he definitely didn't think his visit would change the course of his life, and of many others.

During the hours he and his group spent on the island, Dr. Jimenez began to feel a strong connection to the battle. It was almost as if the memory of those horrible, yet triumphant weeks remained in the air. Visiting the simple memorials and learning of the heroic deeds that had taken place, he felt a great sense of awe. And it wasn't just for the American heroes. He also felt empathy for the Japanese.

"We went into a couple of the caves that were left more or less intact since 1945. Amazingly, the entrances were still marked with holes from bullets and mortars, and burns from flamethrowers," he said.

The temperature outside was 75 degrees and dry. But the caves were hot from the volcanic activity. He walked ten feet into a tunnel and the temperature climbed to the eighties. Another ten feet and it was 90 degrees. Twenty feet farther it was 110 degrees.

"It was amazing. Like an oven," said Dr. Jimenez. "In there it hit me that the Japanese were just young kids, and they'd been called on to fight for their country just like the American kids. They did what they were told. They dug out those tunnels and spent months in there. How courageous and valiant of them to endure that."

Everywhere he walked there was sulfuric mist rising up from the ground. Pillboxes still sat, almost untouched since the battle. At six o'clock, he stood near the spot on Mount Suribachi where the iconic American flag was raised over Iwo Jima.

"I could almost feel what it must have been like for those brave soldiers," he said.

From up there he could see the dark sand beaches stretching for miles, with soft white surf. The sun was setting and the sulfur smoke was rising. A powerful moment at the edge of nowhere.

"The tour guide told us that for the marines, the beaches were treacherous because the surf was rough and the sand was so very soft, like walking in coffee grounds," said Dr. Jimenez. "I'm thinking it doesn't look that rough."

They drove down to the beach where they were given plastic bags to collect souvenir handfuls of sand. He thought it was a little corny, but he went down to the water anyway. The experience was beyond anything he could have imagined.

"Up close you could tell that surf could rip you up and pull you away in two seconds. It was like, 'Whoa!' " said Dr. Jimenez.

Standing there in the powerful surf, looking at the setting sun, he felt a sensation of falling away so that the concerns of the world—the flight home, his work, the night's hotel— suddenly lost importance and were replaced by a connection to the elements, and the souls of the thousands of marines who had died on the beach.

"Oh my God, I swear I felt the energy of all these men that moment. I realized that this was a once-in-a-lifetime moment. Knowing the courageousness of all who had died there. Just to be sitting on that beach that day was almost an out-of-body experience. All the courage came into that one point."

He reached down, grabbed a handful of sand, and put it in the bag.

"At that moment I realized that I deal with a lot of veterans at the hospital. And it struck me that, gosh, this place is sacred. To a marine you can't get any more sacred than this. And so few marines ever get to see it. So I said to myself, 'Why don't I take this sand and any time that I meet a marine I'll be able to give him a bit of Iwo Jima.' What a gift that would be," he said.

He scooped another handful. Then another. Then he kept adding to the bag, scooping and filling until the gallon bag was ready to burst.

"The other people were looking at me like, 'What the hell?' " he said.

After he returned to San Antonio, his experience on the beach kept running through his mind. He dreamt about it. He bought books on Iwo Jima and learned everything he could. He felt consumed by thoughts of the island, the battle, and the marines who died there. He packed a bit of sand into a little vial and put it in his pocket.

A week after his return he was in his clinic speaking to one of his patients, eighty-year-old Miguel Leal, whom Dr. Jimenez describes as a nice guy.

"He came in feeling great, wearing a three-piece suit, a pencil mustache. Out of the blue, I asked him something about his time in the service."

"The marines," he said.

"No way," I said, thinking of the vial.

"I was in Iwo Jima," he said.

Dr. Jimenez nearly fell off his stool. He told him the story of his recent visit. When the man heard it, he opened up. He said he had hardly spoken of it in the years since 1945. He'd been eighteen years old, a scrawny kid. He described being under fire from all directions. All his buddies getting blown to pieces. Mortars.

"He froze in front of me for a second," Dr. Jimenez said. "Then he told me, 'You know what? At that moment, I didn't care about dying. I was just afraid I was going to lose my mind.' "

A chill went up Dr. Jimenez's spine, and he was flooded with emotion realizing that in his pocket was the greatest gift he could give Mr. Leal for his service—a bottle of the same sand he fought on six decades ago. He pulled out the vial.

"I told him what it was and his jaw dropped. He embraced me and we both started crying," said Dr. Jimenez.

"That sand. That sand. Nobody could understand how hard that sand was on us," Leal said.

That was the first vial of sand Dr. Jimenez gave away. And the man carries it with him everywhere. The doctor and the patient became friends. It's been a cathartic experience for both of them, and they've given talks together to people who are interested in the story of Iwo Jima.

Dr. Jimenez continues to give out vials of sand. Dozens so far. And only to marines.

"They are the ones who appreciate it," said Dr. Jimenez. "What I realized from the whole experience is what our military does for us. Especially the marines."

A small act, for sure. He followed his instincts and affected the lives of many. For that, I call Dr. Jimenez a hero.

Or how about another Austin hero named Julia Cuba, who in 1998 started Troop 1500 on a program called Girl Scouts Beyond Bars. GSBB organizes joint mother-daughter Girl Scout meetings in prisons where mothers are incarcerated. But Troop 1500 goes a few steps further, with Cuba paying close attention to the girls' home lives and school progress. Once a month the girls have group therapy. And the troop helps their mothers do well in prison. According to Cuba, 96 percent of the girls have stayed in school and 98 percent have avoided incarceration. That could be partly due to all the fun they have, with campouts, parties, and regular scout activities like earning badges, wearing uniforms, and, of course, selling delicious cookies. That's heroism for sure.

Just like everyday husband and wife heroes Michael William and Sandra S. Baldwin, who came across a man burning in his car after an accident in Wisconsin and saved his life. Or how about Gary Slutkin, a doctor who fought AIDS in Africa and upon returning to Chicago got the idea that violence, too, might spread like a virus. So he started a group called Cease-Fire that trains gangbangers to be "interrupters" who get in the way of fights, conflicts, and other gang problems. Or Dennis H. Mortan, who took the time to pull over when he drove by a mobile home that was on fire in Pineville, Oregon. He went in and rescued Oma D. Pratt from dying. Or Alexander J. Machado, who rescued Craig Burgholzer from his burning truck on a Delaware road. Jeffrey Allen Connell, who entered Aron E. Wallace's flaming home, crawled along the floor beneath the smoke, and rescued her from the fire. There's Stan Hampl, who donated his forensic dental skills for months as he identified remains of the victims of the 9/11 attacks.

In Sri Lanka, Ranjeevan Xavier responded to the horrible tsunami that killed forty-eight thousand by helping people understand how tsunamis work and what to expect in the future. He also buried over 750 people, organized anti-looting patrols, opened a nursery, a dorm, and a nutrition center, and even staged a kite-flying contest to help the survivors. Or Oscar Gonzalez, who intervened to help a U.S. Postal Service mail carrier in Las Vegas who was about to be attacked by a man who was irate over not receiving his welfare check. And I can never forget the men and women of Bangor, Maine, many of them veterans, who greet returning troops with a friendly smile and a platter of cookies.

⁂

The other day I was walking home from work, along Central Park, when an elderly homeless man, sitting on a piece of cardboard, asked me for some money. He was filthy, one of thousands of homeless people in the city. I was in a hurry, headed to the gym. It's possible that at some other time in my life I would have passed him by. But now that I spend my days immersed in my *What Would You Do?* television series, documenting the foibles and heroics of everyday people, I am more cognizant of the world around me. (Or maybe I'm just nervous about the hidden cameras that might be lurking in the tree-tops!) And that's a good thing. So I stopped and chatted with the man for a moment about the day, his life. I wound up buy-ing him some coffee and a burger. Not a big deal, at all. It cost me fifteen minutes and six bucks. But he thanked me with a smile and a gleam in his eyes. It got me thinking about how much more I can do—how much more we can all do—to im-prove our world, every day.

The late Peter Jennings was one of the people I've most admired in my life. He was a great journalist, anchorman, and my greatest role model. He was wealthy and powerful, and didn't have to stoop to help anyone. But he did. Few people know that about him. Even as he struggled with cancer, Peter spent many of his nights riding in a van, delivering meals and blankets, giving money and giving of himself to the homeless and the hungry in New York City.

Now, there's a hero.

"Life is not so short but that there is always
time enough for courtesy."

—Ralph Waldo Emerson

There have been so many other heroes in my life. Like the crew that helped me cover the wars in Central America during the 1980s. They risked their lives every day so that I could get the news back to our viewers. My producer was even taken hostage in Panama during the troubles there.

As a network correspondent for over thirty years, I've covered some huge stories. When there's a war, famine, or other disaster, reporters are called upon to get the stories to their viewers. But even when you're working in the midst of tragedy, you remain a person, with feelings and compassion. I've been blessed with the opportunity to help others in the midst of some of the greatest human tragedies. But I don't think I've done anything exceptional. Thanks to the good lessons my mom taught me, the great example my father set, and the guidance and goodwill of so many other people over the years, I've been able to respond in small ways when I could to help someone out. But really, who wouldn't hand his satellite phone over to an American soldier in Iraq so he could check in with his family back in the States? I did, but wouldn't you do the same?

When I was doing a story about "Brothers to the Rescue," a group of Cuban-American volunteers who spend their days flying over the Florida Straits, those ninety miles between Key West and Cuba, looking for rafters fleeing Castro, we came across a raft floundering in the sea. It had been cobbled together from inner tubes and wood, pieces of boats, Styrofoam, whatever, and it was sinking with seven people on board. Three generations of Cubans who had been desperate for freedom and now they were desperate to live. We notified the

Coast Guard but they were too far away to respond. So we came alongside the raft and I helped pull the people from the choppy sea. Dangerous. Scary. And something we did absolutely without a second thought. It was one of those wild experiences. We ferried them back to Key West, where the authorities took over and eventually allowed them to stay in the U.S. There was the time I was reporting on a devastating Texas tornado when I gave my bottle of water and turkey sandwich to a man who had lost everything. A small act, yes. But not to that man who was hungry and needed compassion.

We all have these precious opportunities, every day, to act in a way that will make our society a better place. Let's open our heart to them and act heroically. All of us. Right now.

Ordinary People, Extraordinary Choices
You Make the Call!

You're at the movies with some friends. Since you arrived early you go out to the concession stand and buy popcorn and drinks. While walking back you see a casual friend's fiancé snuggling into the rear row with a young woman who is definitely not the one he's supposed to marry in less than three months. Your jaw drops. You stare. He sees you and tries to pretend nothing has happened. The movie itself is ruined, as you spend the whole time thinking about how heartbroken your friend will be if she finds out. You don't know what to do.

YOU COULD:

A) Take your popcorn, which doesn't taste so good anymore anyway, and dump it all over his head.

B) Take your popcorn and dump it all over *her* head.

C) Text your friend and tell her to join you at the theater.

D) Mind your own business.

You might be surprised to know that I think D is the best option, since it's just a casual friend who is being betrayed. You might not really know the whole story and getting involved in someone else's love life can be a pretty tricky maneuver. If it were your best friend getting cheated on, then telling her would be the best choice. But clearly, C's not the way to do it. And A and B, while fun, would just leave a bunch of popcorn on the floor for someone else to clean up—why do that to a stranger?

CHAPTER THIRTEEN

Our Hall of Heroes

It's hard to say if all the members of the Hall of Heroes would look approvingly upon their inclusion here. For those who did their hero work in relative anonymity, the knowledge would more likely produce a humble laugh than a proud donning of sashes and crowns of laurel. These people did not seek fame, but it came to them in the honorable and courageous decisions they made in everyday life.

Luckily, we do not have to match that humility in our praise of these worthy individuals, not intended as an exhaustive list but a reminder of bravery. Their sacrifices, whether in the briefest of moments or the perseverance of a lifetime, unite us in the recognition and celebration of human excellence. They did not hide; they did not give up, even when no one would have blamed them for doing so. We honor their efforts, we aspire to be more like them, and, most important, we thank them for inspiring us to greatness.

THE FEARLESS

- Wesley Autrey, Subway Hero
- Terek Beckman and Steven Haws, Rescuers
- Todd Beamer, 9/11 Passenger

THE DETERMINED

- Irena Sendler, Social Worker and Resistance Leader
- Dick and Rick Hoyt, Athletes and Activists
- Aung San Suu Kyi, Pro-Democracy Activist
- Samantha Power, Journalist and Adviser

THE REVOLUTIONARIES

- Norman Borlaug, Agronomist
- Harvey Milk, Politician and Gay Rights Activist
- Hector Garcia, World War II Veteran, Surgeon, Civil Rights Advocate

THE FAITHFUL

- Dr. Rob Boll, Emergency Surgeon
- Dorothy Stang, Sister of the Order of Notre Dame de Namur, Workers Rights Activist, Environmentalist
- Oscar Romero, Bishop and Human Rights Activist

THE PRACTICAL RADICALS

- Muhammad Yunus, Economist
- Adam Werbach, Environmental Activist
- William McDonough, Designer

THE EDUCATORS

- Bunker Roy, Educator
- Wendy Kopp, Founder
- Osceola McCarty, Scholarship Endower

THE LITTLEST HEROES

- Nojoud Muhammad Nasser, Feminist Hero
- Derrionna Adams, Big Sister of the Year
- Lin Hao, Quake Rescuer
- Iqbal Masih, Children's Rights Activist
- Craig Kielburger, Children's Rights Advocate

The Fearless

They don't have secret identities, arch-nemeses, or overly clingy active wear, but make no mistake—these are our *superheroes. They step in and risk their own lives to take care of us when we need it the most. The individuals profiled here are the stuff of legends and bedtime stories.*

◀ WESLEY AUTREY

For utter selfless bravery and kindness to strangers, it is difficult to think of a more worthy example than Wesley Autrey, the subway hero. While taking his two daughters home in early January 2007, Autrey witnessed a young man, Cameron Hollopeter, suffering a seizure on the platform of the downtown No. 1 train in New York City. Cameron fell onto the tracks as the train roared into the station, and Autrey had only a heartbeat to decide. He dove onto the tracks, covering Cameron with his own body as the train ground to a halt above them. He managed to call up to the platform to make sure somebody told his little girls that their daddy was all right.

The extraordinary events of that day are belied by Navy veteran Autrey's calm and humble statement to the *New York Times* following the event, "I don't feel like I did something spectacular; I just saw someone who needed help. . . . I did what I felt was right."

◀ TEREK BECKMAN AND STEVEN HAWS

There is cold, and then there is Idaho Falls, Idaho, cold. Low temperatures in the long winters there reach the teens—on a good day. The icily beautiful Snake River, thawing slightly on a mid-February day in 2007, along with the falls, was a winter wonderland. For Terek Beckman, a young man working two jobs to save for a new mortgage, and Steven Haws, a man on his way to work, it would prove a life- and character-defining morning.

Leslie Watson and her four-year-old daughter had been driving on the road that skirts the river in Watson's SUV. Reports on the how and why differ but the automobile swerved off the road and plunged over the falls and into the river. Bystanders began screaming. At that temperature and with the powerful undertow from the man-made falls, Beckman and Haws knew the Watsons had a precious few moments before they would freeze or drown. With little regard for their own safety, Beckman and Haws lowered themselves into the hypothermia-inducing slush and were able to pull the Watsons to safety. Police Chief J. Kent Livsey was quoted as saying, "For these guys to go out across the ice with no idea whether it was thick or thin was absolutely heroic."

Steven Haws had a different take on it. He told the *Idaho Post Falls Register*, "To me, it's kind of embarrassing. I never thought of myself as a hero, I just thought of myself as another person who did the right thing."

TODD BEAMER

In the aftermath of 9/11, the list of heroes was almost too long to fathom. Firefighters, police, and citizens of every stripe, from every background imaginable, and of every political and religious inclination were lost on that day. The honoring of Todd Beamer on these pages is a tribute to everyone who acted with such fierce bravery in the face of unspeakable horror.

Beamer was a passenger on United 93. He was an account manager at Oracle and had a wife, Lisa, two sons, and a daughter who was born four months after the attacks. Trying to contact help on board the flight he reached a customer service representative, and told her about the horrors unfolding on the plane. He also told her how he was planning to lead a group of passengers to try and wrest control of the airplane away from the hijackers.

The Determined

It's impossible to overestimate the collective good that emerges from those who are presented with a terrible situation and who, with quiet resolve, work and work and work until they have manifested that change. Even when the odds seem insurmountable, the following individuals refused to back down.

IRENA SENDLER

Can you imagine the magnitude of responsibility felt by those who attempted to save children from the vicious Nazi genocide during the Holocaust? For the vast majority of us who will be spared duties even approaching that level of significance, we can probably only get at the surface. Irena Sendler, a Polish social worker, was responsible for a brilliant, incredibly risky plan that saved the lives of Jewish children in Poland from almost certain death in concentration camps. Between 1940 and 1943, commanding a brigade of like-minded citizens, she smuggled some twenty-five hundred children out of the Warsaw ghetto using a multitude of ruses. She claimed some of the children were infected with Typhus, others were snuck out in parcels, boxes, disguises or even *body bags* right under the noses of the Nazi guards. The children were adopted by Polish citizens or placed in Polish orphanages. Sendler kept the records of the children's true identities in the hope that one day the families could be reunited. Eventually, she was arrested by the Nazis, tortured by the Gestapo, and sentenced to death.

But Irena never revealed any information about her work or the identities of the children. This clever woman escaped from the Nazi prison. Before Sendler was taken away, a quick-thinking associate hid the identity information in her undergarments when Sendler's house was searched, then buried the records in a garden.

Sadly, for many of these children, the day their parents made the brave decision to leave them entrusted to Irena Sendler were the last times they would see each other. After the war, Sendler continued her social work, sometimes with children she had rescued. In 1965, she was honored with the Yad Vashem's "Righteous Gentile" award. She lived the rest of her life in relative obscurity, in her elder years cared for by Elzibieta Ficowska, a woman Sendler had smuggled out in a wooden box when Elzibieta was six months old. Later nominated for the Nobel Peace Prize, Sendler explained, "I was taught that if you see a person drowning, you must jump into the water to save them, whether you can swim or not." She later went on to say, "We who were rescuing children are not some kind of heroes. That term irritates me greatly. The opposite is true—I continue to have qualms of conscience that I did so little. I could have done more. This regret will follow me to my death."

≪ DICK AND RICK HOYT

Marathoners are a curious breed. Like fiction writers and assassins, they tend to be a solitary bunch when hard at work, and their chosen sport requires infinite tolerance of their own thoughts, motivations, and demons. It can be difficult to chat when you need every ounce of oxygen you can draw to pump your arms and legs. Marathons are not, by definition, a sport that relies heavily on teamwork. Unless, that is, you are Dick and Rick Hoyt.

Forty-six years ago, Dick Hoyt and his wife were new parents with a special-needs child—well before that phrase was in use. Rick Hoyt's inability to move on his own or speak had the doctors convinced he was a vegetable, and they encouraged the Hoyts to stick him in an institution and move on with their lives. Instead, they fought for the son they loved so much, unconditionally. They knew he was just as intelligent as their other children, even if he had no way to express himself. Working with his parents and researchers who developed special software to help him communicate, Rick graduated from college, they climbed mountains (once, as Dick carried his son up Mount Monadnock he heard passersby whispering, "He's going up to the mountain to sacrifice his son!"), and after guerrilla entries into the first couple of races they attempted, became some of the Boston Marathon's most beloved entrants. They consider themselves the closest of teams, each rooting for the other more than he knows how to root for himself.

"Rick and I are a team, and not just on the roads. We're talking to the schools, telling our story, and telling these kids—some of whom are on alcohol and drugs and cigarettes—that they can do anything they want for themselves."

AUNG SAN SUU KYI

In a fearsome military dictatorship, oftentimes it is a reasonable choice to try to keep one's head down and hope for the best. With no guarantee of fair trial, freedom of speech, or protection from violent or unwarranted imprisonment, survival is a goal in itself. Especially when your country is being held hostage. Aung San Suu Kyi is a different sort of prisoner. A Nobel Peace Prize laureate, she has been under house arrest by the Myanmar (formerly Burma) government almost constantly for eighteen years. In May 2008, her arrest was sustained for another year.

She was born in 1945 to a prominent general, a man described as the "father of Burma." When she was a child, he was assassinated and she was raised primarily by her mother, and educated outside of Burma. Her Theravadic Buddhism stresses nonviolence and, inspired by Mahatma Ghandi, she entered politics and publicly called for a democratic government. Her election to prime minister in 1990—under her National League for Democracy party—was denied by the military junta, and she was imprisoned shortly thereafter.

Her husband, Michael Aris, was a citizen of the United

Kingdom. He was diagnosed with prostate cancer and was refused a visa to visit his wife before he passed away. But Suu
Kyi refused to surrender or leave. She would not back down,
she was not afraid. "It is not power that corrupts but fear. Fear
of losing power corrupts those who wield it and fear of the
scourge of power corrupts those who are subject to it."

SAMANTHA POWER

In this age of New Media—blogs, Twittering, twenty-four-
hour cable news—the flood of information we receive is as
overwhelming as it is easy to turn off, to ignore. Especially
when that news is horror stories from half a world away (come
to think of it, it's actually quite easy to ignore the horror stories in our own backyard, as well). Traditional journalism
doesn't pay particularly well, yet there are still those who force
us, gently, to hear the truth.

Samantha Power was born in Ireland and moved to the
States when she was nine. She made her first, life-changing
trip as a journalist to Bosnia when she was twenty-three, an
age when most of us are still trying to find our way out of the
adult-adolescent limbo. Since that time, she has traveled and
written and spoken extensively about the horrors she has witnessed in places like Bosnia, the Sudan, Rwanda, Cambodia,
and Iraq, and the failure of American foreign policy in these
situations. She won a Pulitzer Prize for her groundbreaking
book, *A Problem from Hell.*

Her willingness to be where no one else wants to even think about, much less go, and report back about those who need our help the very most is overwhelming.

In 2004, she told the *Atlanta Journal-Constitution,* "People in the world notice the selective application of principles. The United States has to be at the vanguard of human rights and dignity, but it will not be until it stops applying these principles in an a la carte fashion."

The Revolutionaries

We all want to change the world. These people actually did. They have little in common with each other, save for the fact that without them, the world would be a worse place to live. Some were life-savers on a global scale, others were change agents in lesser arenas, but they all reformed a broken system, they all knew they could make things better.

NORMAN BORLAUG

For those who have never heard of him, it's hard to give Norman Borlaug a decent introduction. He's the winner of a Nobel Peace Prize. He has also won the Presidential Medal of Freedom and the Congressional Gold Medal. Norman Borlaug, the founder of the Green Revolution, is personally responsible for saving the lives of approximately one billion people. Yes, one *billion*. The enormity and significance of his work—for the development of high-yield, disease-resistant agriculture primarily used to feed the world's poor—cannot be overstated.

Borlaug was born in Iowa in 1931. His primary education was modest, and he recalls being influenced by the misery he witnessed during the Dust Bowl. His belief that to end human misery was a mission to feed the belly led to brilliant discoveries in plant genetics.

It seems a gross oversight that we do not all celebrate Norman Borlaug Day, see children proudly adorned in Norman Borlaug Halloween costumes, or name our babies after him. Yet this humble man probably wouldn't have it any other way. He has better things to do. The now ninety-four-year-old told Peter Jennings in 2004, "I hope I can continue to work and be at least acceptably productive and die with my boots on, working."

HARVEY MILK

When we watch those who are the first to breach the barriers of gender, race, class, and sexual orientation in our society, there are moments of both thrilling glory and exhausting heartbreak. Harvey Milk, the first "openly gay man elected to any substantial public office in the history of the planet," according to *Time* magazine, was a man of genuine courage and, by all accounts, a wonderful sense of humor. His election to city supervisor of San Francisco was a beacon of hope to the disenfranchised everywhere, and he remains a hero, especially to gay, lesbian, bisexual, and transgender youth around the world.

Milk was assassinated in 1978 at the hands of Dan White, a disgruntled city employee who got minimal time using the infamous "Twinkie Defense": his counsel maintained White was not a homophobe and attempted to blame the murder on the consumption of a large amount of junk food. Following the outrage that came from the trial, diminished capacity was outlawed as a defense in the state of California.

Milk's legacy lives on, most notably in the schools and youth organizations that bear his name. Understanding that his life and commitment to equality could possibly end in his death, he made this point clearly in an audio recording: "If a bullet should enter my brain, let that bullet destroy every closed door."

HECTOR GARCIA

A core belief in the equality, and the will to fight for it, is the basis of every civil rights movement and piece of legislation on the books. Without those who fight, there are very few among us who would not be utterly subject to a perceived superior.

Most people will never hear the name Hector Garcia, including those for whom he advocated. Born in Mexico, Garcia moved to the United States and joined the army. He got his medical degree and shortly thereafter volunteered for combat duty. He became a major in the army, also earning a Bronze Star.

When he returned to Texas, he created the American GI Forum as a social and political network that fought for the rights of Latinos—veterans, migrant workers, and everyone else who came to "Dr. Hector" for help. His legacy is one of change and honor. He was instrumental in the fight to desegregate and educate. He gave free medical attention to those who needed it, and was known as a man of impeachable integrity. His spirit lives on in his lifetime motto, "Education is our freedom, and freedom is everybody's business."

The Faithful

There can be no doubt that many of the most beautiful and healing humanitarians the world has known have drawn their strength and purpose from their spiritual beliefs. We look no further than Gandhi, Dr. Martin Luther King Jr., Mother Teresa—the list is truly endless. To these giants, we add the following faithful.

DR. ROB BOLL

It's hard for any of us to predict how we might handle ourselves in a situation that requires us to harness all our mental strength and utilize nimble fingers under grave stress. For Dr. Rob Boll, a fifty-two-year-old family practitioner in Mokena, Illinois, he now has his answer: with amazing grace. Sitting down to a church dinner of turkey and apple pie, Colleen Rohrer's cry of "Help!" from across the room jolted him out of his seat. Her mother-in-law was choking and after an attempt to remove the object from her throat proved fruitless, Dr. Boll realized the only way to save her life was to perform an emergency tracheotomy. He'd never performed one before, and the last time he'd *seen* one was twenty years prior. His heart pounded in his chest.

Working with Colleen "just like a surgical team," he was able to use a paring knife, then a switchblade, then a miraculously present tracheotomy tube and manual resuscitator bag to revive and stabilize the woman before EMT technicians took over. In *Reader's Digest* Dr. Boll reflected, "I'm not terribly religious . . . but I know now that God goes to turkey dinners at churches. To take a doctor who only half knows what he's doing and give him the right tools—I don't know how I recalled what I needed to do. To me, there's no explanation but divine intervention."

◀ SISTER DOROTHY STANG

It is sometimes the case that the most outwardly meek among us conceal within themselves profound reserves of heavy-duty moxie. Such was the case with a rural nun named Sister Dorothy Stang, born in Dayton in 1931 with, by all accounts, strength and sass to last two lifetimes. Her childhood best friend, Sister Joan Krimm, laughs at the memory of two teenagers smoking purloined cigars and chatting innocently about entering the convent and saving the world.

Moving to Coroata, Brazil, in 1966, and later deeper into the Amazon to minister to peasant farmers lured there to work along the Amazon highway, Stang finally settled in the state of Para. Land disputes in this area of Brazil end frequently in violence and murder. Stang fearlessly stood up to wealthy landowners hell-bent on destroying the delicate forest for cattle ranching, trampling any peasants or clergy that stood in their way. Aided by the Pastoral Land Commission, a part of the Catholic Church that advocates on behalf of rural workers, she continued her ministry and outspoken criticism of these practices. The commission estimates as many as eight hundred "settlers, union members and priests have been killed in Para over the last thirty years." Stang received multiple death threats, laughing them off to her worried friends and family.

On February 12, 2005, Sister Stang was murdered in a contract killing. Attempting to reason with her murderers proved fruitless, but she held fast to her Bible stating, "This is my weapon." She quoted from the Bible before being shot. "Blessed are they who hunger and thirst for justice, for they shall be satisfied."

BISHOP OSCAR ROMERO

Bespectacled, bookish Oscar Romero's initial appointment to the position of Archbishop of San Salvador was devastating to the priests who had been hoping a non-conservative crusading bishop would be appointed in the wake of the Liberation Theology movement. Would their prayers for a progressive leader to help end the violence, poverty, and political oppression in El Salvador ever be heard? He did not disabuse them of the notion that he would not take sides. He had no compulsion to be political. Immediately, that is.

Bishop Romero, moved to action when a priest, Rutilio Grande, was assassinated, went on to become the most outspoken and crusading leader the Church in Central America had ever known. He worked with the poor, he fought against injustice, and he did it all. His assassination in May 1980 by right-wing extremists—as he was saying Mass—was the most gruesome and heartbreaking event to happen to a people who were used to outrage, sadness, and fear. His funeral was but another excuse for the death squads to rain violence down on the mourners and plunge the country back into a period of darkness.

Romero once wrote in his diary, "In recent days the Lord has inspired in me a great desire for holiness. . . . I have been thinking of how far a soul can ascend if it lets itself be possessed entirely by God." It seems there would be no limit.

The Practical Radicals

There are more glamorous ways to make hay than the modes used by these practical radicals. Surely a nationally televised hunger strike, an orphan photo-op, or a noisy protest makes for sexier media coverage. Our practical radicals politely declined the splashier modes of do-gooding in favor of a more linear cerebral strategy to get their work done.

ADAM WERBACH

Born about the same time as the first Earth Day was celebrated, Adam Werbach became, at twenty-three, the youngest president of the Sierra Club. He was hip, young, and wildly determined—green in more ways than one. Twelve years later, he is as tenacious as ever, but his message has changed.

As part of a new generation of activists and businesspeople who see a market in sustainability and stewardship of the planet, Werbach has spearheaded campaigns from former eco-villains like Wal-Mart. He saw in them the potential to reach millions more than any letter-writing campaign could ever hope to accomplish. By working with, instead of against, the entrenched retail behemoths, he and his former company, Act Now (it was absorbed by advertising giant Saatchi and Saatchi), effect massive amounts of change, while making money and pleasing customers. The *New York Times* quoted him as saying, "We've spent too much time saying, 'Do this because the polar bears are dying,'" he says. "Instead, we need to say, 'Do this because it brings about success and happiness in our businesses and families.'"

◀ WILLIAM MCDONOUGH

It might seem a little odd that we choose to call William McDonough, an environmental designer, a hero. He is not one in the traditional sense but right now seems the best time ever for the untraditional hero. A pioneer of the green movement and green architecture, he is a visionary of unusual intellectual flexibility. He manipulates nature and man-made materials to provide sustainable buildings—most notably the "living roof" on the Ford plant in Michigan.

His sensibility is best summed up in the "cradle-to-cradle" mentality he espouses. Inventing new ways of recycling the old bridges the gap between beauty and functionality, and he is relentless in his drive to make sustainability a reality everywhere.

"It means that nothing has to be junked. It means life after life."

The Educators

As an investment in human capital, there is nothing that returns like education. The fastest route to democracy, universal suffrage, equal rights, and so many of the values we hold fast and dear is education. It's often a thankless task, but those we salute have taken to it with fortitude, ingenuity, and love.

BUNKER ROY

Education, as any educator will tell you, is decidedly not a one-size-fits-all endeavor. Educational fads—everything from "new" math to laptops-for-every-child mentalities—come and go. Predicting the new best way to teach is a difficult task, especially when faced with a system that simply isn't working.

With little tolerance for formal education, bureaucracy, and top-down programs to combat poverty, Sanjit "Bunker" Roy is something of an educational maverick. He is an Indian activist, in possession of the swanky degrees he disdains, who built his institution, Barefoot College, to liberate the rural poor in India from dependency on anyone but themselves. The college, which has instructed over fifteen thousand boys and girls in "barefoot" economics, technology, and engineering, is predicated on the belief that poverty is eliminated, people are made self-sufficient, gender equality is achieved, and the environment is protected when, and only when, "practical knowledge and skills, rather than paper qualifications" are implemented into the communities that need them the most.

Elegance in implementation is vital to Roy. "More needs to be learnt and unlearnt from the growing corps of social entrepreneurs. These entrepreneurs are the new activists, but because they live and work with poor communities, driving change from the bottom upwards, their solutions to poverty are often simple, practical, and rooted in traditional forms of working."

◁ WENDY KOPP

With some five thousand member teachers instructing close to half a million needy students around the country, Wendy Kopp's Teach for America program is a big idea with curious roots. Contemplating her upcoming senior thesis at Princeton, Kopp was decidedly uninspired, and she knew other students who felt the same way. She wanted to make a difference after graduation but could not find an outlet that suited her. So she created one.

Drawing on Kennedy's Peace Corps as a model for her program, Teach for America was born. She desperately wanted to teach children in failing schools. Lacking funding, Kopp decided to go big—she pestered Ross Perot until he wrote her a check for $500,000. Teach for America has grown into a well-funded, highly regarded institution. They recruit and train teachers who would be in demand in any field they chose to enter. Kopp is sanguine about the future. "Teach for America is not going to solve all the problems in education, but we have learned so much that I feel can help catalyze change in the whole system."

OSCEOLA MCCARTY

The transformative power of education is one of the few forces in our society that reaches across gender, race, class, and age lines. When the opportunity to receive a decent education vanishes, or was never there to begin with, every one of us suffers as a result. For Osceola McCarty, an elderly woman in Hattiesburg, Mississippi, her chance was lost when a relative needed nursing, forcing her to quit school in the sixth grade. McCarty went immediately from attendant to full-time work, toiling as a washerwoman for nearly seventy-five years; she found electric washing machines to be ersatz inconveniences and did all her laundering work by hand. She never married and never had children.

When it came time to retire, McCarty, who had lived frugally her entire life, had $300,000 in her retirement fund. For many, that would have meant a more luxurious retirement, perhaps a new house or a fancy automobile, but she had other ideas in mind. She phoned the University of Mississippi in Hattiesburg and informed them she would like to endow a scholarship for African-American students in the area. She donated half of her money.

It's an interesting way to think about the scale of her gift—*half* of everything she owned so that kids in her community would not have to endure the backbreaking labor that she did. But McCarty chose to see her scholarship as a contribution to the community that she belonged to—education as investment in the future for everyone. When asked by a *People* magazine reporter why she didn't keep the money for herself, she replied with a smile, "I am spending it on myself."

The Littlest Heroes

The young people profiled here are the most heartwarming and heartbreaking examples of heroes we can find. With childlike determination that should be the envy of all adults, these kids stood up for themselves and for each other, they made choices and acted bravely in ways that many adults will never match. We eagerly await all they will do next.

≼ NOJOUD MUHAMMAD NASSER

In Yemen, one of the most pitiless places in the world to be a woman, the life of a little girl can be even more dangerous. To be *a little girl* challenging the patriarchy—that is an astounding act of bravery. When she was eight years old, Nojoud Muhammad Nasser was married off—by her father—to a thirty-year-old man. Unaware of what being a "wife" entailed, Nojoud was the victim of repeated violence and sexual abuse. As reported in the *Yemen Times*, before her marriage she had begged to be spared, but her father insisted that if she did not comply, she would be raped and "no law and no sheikh would help [her]." She did not intend to keep it that way.

In early April 2008, tiny Nojoud arrived unaccompanied (her parents and an aunt had all refused to help her) at a court in Sana'a and demanded prosecution for her father and her

husband. Though Yemeni law allows for the sanctioned marriage of those younger than fifteen and though she was technically too young to prosecute, the judge ruled in her favor, the
divorce was granted, and the judge ordered the arrests of both
her father and husband. Asked about her brave challenge,
Nojoud told the reporter that she just wanted to have "a re-
spectful life." She has certainly earned it.

◀ DERRIONNA ADAMS

The newly minted Firefighter No. 60 of East St. Louis, Illinois, is one Derrionna Adams, a twelve-year-old girl who
saved the lives of her brothers and sisters during a fire that
destroyed every material possession the family owned—but
nothing more. When her little sister woke Derrionna up
after smelling smoke, Derrionna immediately took charge.
Breaking out a window and lining up her siblings, she orches-
trated their safe delivery outside with poise and calm enviable
at any age.

Bravery must run in this family. Derrionna's nine-year-old
brother, Deveontae Neal, would not leap to safety until he was
sure his little sister, Bernicia, was safe. Unaware his baby sister had slept in a different room that night, Deveontae ran
back into the fire to save her, ensuring his own safety only
when he knew she was outside the rapidly engulfed house.

Derrionna told the *St. Louis Post-Dispatch* that "she didn't
feel like a hero." All she did, in fact, was pay attention to the

lessons learned at home. "Our momma told us we have to look out for each other."

⬤ LIN HAO

The first thing you notice about little Lin Hao, wildly famous around the world as Yao Ming's Olympic buddy in Beijing, is that the nine-year-old is disarmingly cute. Perched upon Yao's massive shoulders or serenely taking in the glory-filled walk around the track at the Bird's Nest, he stole the show—a difficult feat considering the phenomenal spectacle that was the Opening Ceremonies. But as Yao and Hao marched and waved and beamed to their proud nation, it was immediately apparent he was wounded. At least one billion people around the world collectively teared up as television announcers in a multitude of languages told his story.

On May 12, 2008, a massive tremor shook the Sichuan province of China. Hao, who was a second-grader at the Yuzixi Primary School in Yingxiu, Wenchuan County—the epicenter of the quake—was in his class of thirty when the quake occurred. His school collapsed. He was injured but still managed to find two classmates and pull them out of the rubble. Hours later, rescue workers followed the sound of his singing—he was trying to cheer up those still trapped—and when they took him to the doctor he insisted his classmates be treated first.

We're always trying to teach our kids about responsibility.

Sometimes, just investing them with that responsibility can prove more effective than a thousand lectures. This young man simply stated, "I was the squad leader, it was my job to look after my classmates."

◀ IQBAL MASIH

It is difficult to write about Iqbal Masih. It is difficult to think of him without feeling like we may never be able to do enough good to make up for the amount of greed, corruption, malice, and brutality that we encounter in this world. Iqbal was just four years old when he was sold into slavery to Pakistani carpet-makers. He spent the next six years of his life—half of it, as it would turn out—shackled to a loom before escaping with the aid of the Bonded Labor Liberation Front of Pakistan. Upon his escape, he allegedly owed the manufacturers an amount that would have taken him thirty-five years to pay off—he had been earning approximately three cents a day. He began school and worked on behalf of BLLF, eventually helping to free some three thousand children from the bonds of enforced labor.

Iqbal received death threats from the so-called "Carpet Mafia," but he continued with his work, becoming an outspoken critic of the malicious treatment he and the other children received. He won humanitarian awards and planned to use the prize money to go to law school. On April 16, 1995, he was gunned down near Lahore, believed by many to be the victim of the vengeance-minded cabal of carpet manufacturers that young Iqbal had refused to fear. But from his incredible sacrifice came hope, and those who were and continued to be inspired by Iqbal have taken up the cause under his name. Iqbal had another name on his mind as inspiration. Before being killed, he spoke to Peter Jennings of ABC News: "I would like to do what Abraham Lincoln did in this country. I'd like to do it in Pakistan."

CRAIG KIELBURGER

It's unbelievably easy to feel inadequate and even easier to find people to compare ourselves to—on television, at work or school, even in our own families—who make us feel even worse. There's always someone younger, trimmer, richer, or lovelier than we are, and it can be difficult to keep ourselves from the disgruntled suspicion that we, in fact, deserve so much more.

It is the rare individual who is so infuriated by comparing his life to another that he mounts a colossal effort to change the circumstances that led to the discrepancy. Even rarer still when that individual is twelve years old, when he is comparing his unbelievable good fortune to those who were born with nothing.

Free the Children was the brainchild of Craig Kielburger, a young man so moved by the heroism and slaying of Iqbal Masih—a twelve-year-old, just like himself—that he immediately enlisted thirty other children to see what they could do about that grave injustice. According to their website, "Free the Children is the world's largest network of children helping children through education, with more than one million youth involved in our innovative education and development programs in forty-five countries." He has continued this crusade into adulthood—travelling, speaking, relentlessly advocating for those who could not fight for themselves.

The explosive response was not originally what Craig had anticipated. Hoping to raise $10,000 on a night when his speech brought down the house and brought in $150,000 to combat Third World exploitation of children, his onstage reaction was as genuine as they come. As the donations rolled in, he addressed the crowd, "I think I'm going to faint."

Acknowledgments

It would be impossible to properly thank everyone who contributed to this book, or to all the great stories I've reported at ABC News. You know who you are. But I feel compelled to single out a few people:

Chris Whipple, my great friend and the amazingly creative Series Producer of *What Would You Do?*, who came up with the idea of a "Candid Camera of Ethics"—and would not take no for an answer until ABC News made it a series in its own right. And, who turns out to be as gifted with words on the printed page as he is with our *WWYD?* scripts.

To my friend and colleague Diane Sawyer who, through example, never ceases to inspire.

Paul Julian, much more than my agent, a loyal best friend who's never wavered in his support for me through the good times (and bad?) . . . and the toughest times.

Lisa Queen, who always believed in this book and guided me through the world of book publishing.

Stephen Williams, my partner in writing this book, who went out in the field and chronicled the lives of so many of our heroes.

Rene Alegria, my editor at HarperCollins/Rayo books, who took a vague notion and turned it into a brilliant concept for a book.

David Sloan, Executive Producer of *PrimeTime* and *20/20*, who has been unfailingly creative, supportive—and who was smart enough to recognize a promising new franchise when he saw one.

Robert Lange, Broadcast Producer of *PrimeTime* and *What Would You Do?*, a good friend and wise producer with a keen eye for telling stories.

Dr. Carrie Keating, Professor of Psychology at Colgate University, for her endless assistance in the formulation of our *What Would You Do?* scenarios and for her brilliant commentary and analysis.

Dr. Jack Dovidio, Psychology Professor, Yale University, for his expert analysis.

David Westin, President, ABC News, for his guidance and support and for allowing me to cover the world for ABC News.

Dave Davis, Vice-President, ABC News, for believing and standing by this book.

Phyllis McGrady, Vice President of ABC News, former Executive Producer of *PrimeTime*, for her years of friendship and for allowing me to "shine the light of journalism on the darkest corners of the world."

Danielle Baum, our creative and energetic Senior Producer.

Charnee Perez, who did a terrific job researching heroes, an almost endless task.

Emma Jade Brazier, who got the ball rolling on all our research.

What Would You Do?'s team of producers, directors, support staff, cameramen, and editors—who may be the most talented in the TV news business.

Robert Campos, my dear friend and brave and dedicated ABC producer responsible for so many of my stories in Central and South America and who, during our coverage of the U.S. invasion of Panama in 1989, was kidnapped while in pursuit of the story . . . (and thankfully, later released).

Joe LoMonaco and Steven Blanco, the award-winning ABC camera crew who never left my side, literally dodging bullets and bombs during the turbulent '80s in Latin America, all the while bringing tremendous sensitivity to all our stories.

My sisters, Irma and Rosemary, who never let me forget about my wonderful Mexican roots down in San Antonio . . .

They are all heroes of mine . . . in their own, special ways.